JACKIE CHAN
SPECIAL EDITION

Published by Eastern Heroes Publishing
Produced by Rick Baker

Cover Artwork: Crike99art

Design & layout: Tim Hollingsworth
Instagram: 79_design

Printing: Ingramspark

Contributors:

UK
Rick Baker, Michael Nesbitt, Johnny Burnett, Simon Pritchard, Alan Donkin, Matt Routledge, Tim Hollingsworth, Paul Dre.

USA
Jason McNeil

Germany
Thorsten Boose

Special Thanks
Brett Ratner
Andy Cheng
Vincent Lyn

All rights reserved. No part of this publication may be reproduced or transmitted in any or by any means, graphic, electronic or mechanical, including photocopying, recording, taping or any information storage and retrieval system, without prior written permission of the publisher.
© 2021 Eastern Heroes.

Editorial

He we are again with another bumper issue coming in at 120 pages. This was the biggest issue I ever had to compile and also write. But I am proud of this and all the people that contributed to make this such a special issue. Thank you to Brett Ratner for taking time out to talk about the production of "Rush Hour" and to Vincent and Andy for revisiting there memories and their experiences working with "THE LEGEND" that is Jackie Chan. I hope you enjoy this as much as I did putting it together. I would like to think that we can do another special on Jackie and always welcome for people to contact me if they have an interesting story that will be well received within the pages of an "EASTERN HEROES SPECIAL".

Thank you and as always
Keep the Faith

Rick Baker

Contents

4. Cometh The Hour - Brett Ratner
14. Jackie Chan Fanclub
28. Battle Creek Brawl
34. Collecting Japaneses EPs
40. Collecting Japanese Flyers
53. Bud Spencer & Jackie Chan
63. Jackie Chan's Lucky Stars
66. Appreciate the Lobby
73. Poster Story
85. 5 Fingers of Discs
90. That Condor Moment Interview with Vincent Lyn
99. The Professional Collector
102. Andy Cheng: Man on a Mission
107. Half a Loaf of Video CD

COMETH the hour

Exclusive BRETT RATNER Interview

By Rick Baker

"In the beginning the world had flirted with Hong Kong action comedy, But it was not until Jackie Chan came along that we fell in love with it"

Depending on your age, your first glimpse of Jackie Chan in the UK might have been late night cinema, or one of the many Chinese theatres in the States in the late 70s. It might have been that you saw it on video in the 80s, where in the UK 'Rank Video' had released "Drunken Master" and "Snake in the Eagle's Shadow." It might have been "Rumble in the Bronx" or "Drunken Master 2" in the 90s. Or, for the younger readers, their first glimpse of Jackie would more likely have been on DVD, where many of Jackie's films were being released. Toby Russell and I released 12 of the Lo Wei movies on our Eastern Heroes label, and were one of the first companies out the gate mastering those classics onto DVD.

IF AT FIRST YOU DO NOT SUCCEED: TRY, TRY AGAIN

In 1980, Jackie made his US debut with "The Big Brawl," AKA, "Battle Creek Brawl," helmed by "Enter the Dragon" director Robert Clouse. The movie featured much of the same crew, in a search for a new Bruce Lee and follow-up success to the 1973 masterpiece. Whilst it was a moderate success in North America and Hong Kong, The Big Brawl was a box office disappointment, as it performed below expectations in these markets (though it went on to have more success in other Asian and European markets). The film's disappointing performance in North America, however, led to Chan being advised to try supporting roles, such as his turn as the Japanese racing

car driver in "The Cannonball Run" and "Cannonball Run 2." Chan later made another attempt to break into the American market in 1985 with "The Protector," directed by James Glickenhaus. The original Glickenhaus version was a box office failure in North America, while Chan's edited version was a moderate success in Asia. Things took a turn for the better in 1995, when "Rumble in the Bronx" hit American theatres. The movie positioned Jackie as the star, alongside Anita Mui and Françoise Yip. It was directed by Stanley Tong, with action choreographed by both Chan and Tong. Rumble in the Bronx was Jackie's first taste of global success after its worldwide theatrical run, and finally brought Chan into the North American mainstream. The film is set in the Bronx area of New York City, but was filmed in, and around, Vancouver.

It was not until 1998 that one young man's dreams of making a film with Jackie Chan became a reality. The movie was "Rush Hour," and the young man in question Brett Ratner. Taking nearly $250 million at the worldwide box office, "Rush Hour" finally made Jackie Chan a global superstar and made Brett an A-List director. Brett took time out to talk to me. This is his story.

I opened by asking Brett how it all started.

BR: The movie idea was always in the back of my mind, but being a kid making music videos back then, you had to take what you could get. I had been offered a few movies that I had passed on. I was like 25-26 at the time.

RB: So, let's rewind a bit. At what stage did you start to have thoughts about going into the movie industry?

BR: That would be when I was 8 years old. I had seen movies like "Raging Bull," and, of course, I had seen "Enter the Dragon." I loved movies and I knew at the age of 8 that I wanted to become a director. Also, at the age of six I was taking martial arts. I started to take an interest in music, especially rap and hip hop. It was an amalgamation of music, doing martial arts, and loving kung fu films - especially Bruce Lee and Jackie Chan - that inspired me at an early age to have aspirations of becoming a movie director. I would often go to revival cinemas where I would see old kung fu movies. I also watched them when they screened on late night television.

RB: We definitely share similar interests! Did you watch a lot of kung fu movies while you were growing up?

BR: Yes, I always had my eyes glued to the screen while watching martial arts cinema. It was here that I discovered Jackie Chan early on, and he was always in the back of my mind. But then again, I had no control over what my first movie was going to be!

RB: Do you remember the first Jackie Chan movie you saw?

BR: I think it was "Drunken Master." I cannot remember exactly, but I do know that the first kung fu movie that I saw was "Dirty Ho" with Gordon Liu, and then I remember seeing "Thirty-Six Chambers of Shaolin," also starring Gordon Liu. I always remember that movie - it stuck with me - but I only remember certain scenes from "Dirty Ho." I was only eight or nine years old at the time. I also remember "Snake in the Eagle's Shadow" by Woo Ping - it was a great kung fu action comedy.

RB: So, you were now on your path to becoming a director?

BR: As I was wanting to become a director, Miramax and New Line Cinema were beginning to release Hong Kong Jackie Chan movies. I was going to the cinema to see all these Jackie Chan movies, and I started to see what they were trying to do. At home, I watched the Hong Kong versions of those movies, and then I saw the way the studios (meaning Miramax and New Line) edited them, and I felt that they lost the feeling of the films, because they changed all

the music and tried to kind-of 'Americanise' those movies.

RB: I remember that subtitled films were not greatly received back in the day by American audiences, and only the hard-core would go in search of them from their local Chinatowns.

BR: I used to go to home video shops in Chinatown and buy the subtitled versions of these films. Professionally, at the time I was doing the Wu-Tang videos. It was not by accident that I was doing their videos! It was my love of martial arts movies and my love of music and hip-hop that led me to the Wu-tang Clan.

What happened was, I saw what Miramax and New Line were releasing - which in my opinion were bad versions. They were messing up the original intention of the movies for the audience. Those movies were made for Hong Kong audiences. They had a style and existed in a genre unto themselves. Miramax and New Line wanted to release those films theatrically, because they thought there was a few million bucks to be made. Basically, it was those versions of the film that lead me to realise that I could make a movie like "Rush Hour." I could attempt to do everything they were trying to do, but with greater success. They could not pull off their efforts because they were just treating it like an editorial job, or a dubbing job, or a re-mixing job, or a re-scoring job adding American music.

RB: What was the turning point for you?

BR: I saw "Rumble in the Bronx", and it put the nail in the coffin for me. It made me realise that, whoa! Jackie now sees, that his Hong Kong movies are being released in the USA, and building an audience. But remember – it was still a very cult audience watching his movies. His films had been taking maybe four to five million at the box office, so he thought, "Let me make a Hong Kong movie and title it with an American title: Rumble in the Bronx." He did not understand the potentials specifically, but he was right about trying to grab that bigger audience.

RB: Rumble in the Bronx did have some

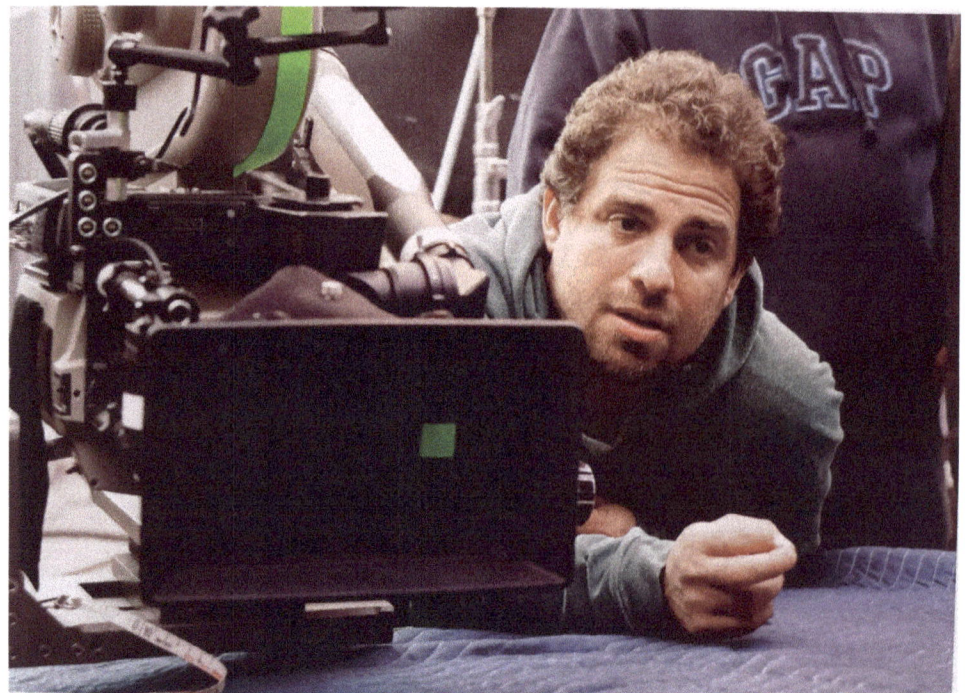

some dramatic action movies in the U.S, and you can see the box office between the action movies that he was doing, and "Rush Hour." It was totally out of whack. Dramas are not big box office. Action comedies, because of "Lethal Weapon," and because of "Beverly Hills Cop," were the biggest genre. They had action, drama AND comedy! And I incorporated Martial arts into that mix.

RB: So "Rush Hour" was no accident?

BR: Rush Hour was no accident! It was created through my observations over years and years. I ended up working with Chris Tucker because I asked him to be in a music video for "Heavy D." I paid Chris $500. He wanted $1000, but I did not have the money. The video went to No1, and I started getting a lot more work, so I mailed him another $500, and for that he never forgot me. After that, he ended up doing "Friday" for which he got $15,000. He then did "Dead Presidents" and then he got offered this movie, "Money Talks." When they were firing the director of "Money Talks," guess whose name Chris put in the hat.

RB: I am going to guess you, Brett?

BR: That's right, because he remembered that I had mailed him the $500 that he must have really needed at the time. "Money Talks" was a kind of buddy movie with Charlie Sheen and Chris Tucker, a "fish out of water" movie just like "Beverly Hills Cop." This was a light bulb moment for me. I thought, 'This is the film I should do.' I really wanted to do "Rush Hour," which wasn't the title in my head at the time, but rather a concept of the movie I wanted to make. I knew that if I had a hit with "Money Talks," even though I couldn't incorporate martial arts into the movie, then it opened doors. So, I decided to do it. I was always planning ahead, so guess what I decided to do? Form a relationship with Lalo Schifrin! I asked him to do the score for "Money Talks," because in the back of my mind I wanted him to do the music for "Rush Hour."

RB: So, the pieces were becoming to come together, Brett?

BR: Yes. This was not an audition, but more of a rehearsal for "Rush Hour." I had a major element on board. Lalo Schifrin knew how to mix Chinese instrumentation with urban grooves. I knew that when "Money Talks" was a hit, the studio (New Line) would say, 'So what

success on its release.

BR: Rumble in the Bronx was the first Hong Kong movie that was released in the States that did 30 million at the box office. So, when the box office return came back, I thought, "Shit! My idea is going to work!" But now I had to create something specific that was not going to be a Hong Kong movie, but was going to have a character from Hong Kong cinema: "Jackie Chan." The biggest star in Hong Kong cinema! I wanted to insert him into a USA genre-centric concept and create a buddy cop movie.

So, you take a Hong Kong character, you put him into a buddy cop formula (which is the Eddie Murphy formula), and then that is going to work like "Gang Busters," which is the reverse of what they did with "Black Rain." They took an American

cop and put him into a Japanese setting. I was taking a Hong Kong cop, bringing him to the US, and putting him with a comedian. I knew that an action comedy would do better than a straight drama. Jet Li had done

do you want to do next?' And basically, they said, 'We will do whatever you want.' I said I had an idea. I wanted to put Jackie Chan and Chris Tucker in a movie together. They told me to go and do it, and the rest is history.

RB: Where did the script come from?
BR: Well, what I did was I found a script. However, it was not written for a black and Chinese guy. The script was called "Rush Hour." It was an action comedy which took place in rush hour traffic. That is why it's called "Rush Hour." Rush hour itself is not really connected to the movie in a major way. The guy in the script says, "What's the problem officer?" and the cop replies, "It's rush hour." That is the only connection to the movie. It was like a background.

RB: What was the original concept?
BR: The original concept was that it was set in rush hour traffic, and it was for two white dudes. So, I adjusted it. I hired Jeff Nathanson who came in and wrote Rush Hour as it existed in my mind - as a buddy cop movie. When I gave it to Jackie, it was not written for a Chinese guy and a black guy. So, he had to read it and imagine that his character was going to be Chinese, and that the other character was going to be a black guy. I had pitched him the idea. I met with Mark Odesky, who was the guy who was releasing through "Fine-Line" pictures that were starring Jackie Chan. I said, 'I need your help! New Line is telling me that I can make this movie, but I've got to get Jackie Chan to be in it! That is the goal!' So, he said, 'Ok, these are the three things you will want to know. One, Jackie Chan hates American film directors. He had a bad experience on "Cannonball Run." He never wants to work in America, EVER! He also had bad experiences when he did try again. Two, if you meet Jackie, he is not going to tell you whether he likes the idea or not. He is Chinese, he will keep his thoughts to himself very closely. Three, whatever he offers you to eat or drink, you'd better do it, because it an insult to Chinese people if you refuse.'

RB: So, armed with that information, what did you do?
BR: Well, I found him in South Africa filming "Who Am I?" He let me come; I flew 26 hours from LA to South Africa just to have lunch. When I arrived at the airport, Jackie was picking me up. I was so nervous, I just kept saying, "Jackie, I cannot

believe I am here with you." I could see that he was looking at me in the back seat through the rear-view mirror and thinking, "This guy is crazy."
RB: Probably exactly the way I, and any other Jackie fan, would have been for their first meeting, LOL!
BR: We got to the restaurant and he offered me a piece of abalone (abalone is a common name for any of a group of small, to very large, marine gastropod molluscs in the family 'Haliotidae'). It tasted like I was chewing rubber! It's very expensive - like $1000. Then he offered me wine, but I do not drink alcohol. I had to pretend that I was drinking the wine! The abalone, I was spitting into my napkin, because I did not want to insult him. What I told him was, "Jackie, you have been making films since I was born." I was 26 when I met him. I said that I loved his movies, but that things would be different in the US. For instance, take the movie in which he fought Bradley on top of the roof (Gorgeous). I told him that the fight would be different in the United States. His usual fight sequences are like twenty minutes long, but that he would not be allowed to do that in an American movie. He just looked at me. I also told him, "Your villains are faceless, they're just stunt guys" like Andy Cheng or Ken Lo. I explained to him, "You've got to have a real villain, because people love the villain as much as they love the hero." I reassured him. I said, "I know what to do with your movies. I saw "Rumble in the Bronx." I saw how they re-edited all your movies. I know how to make a movie that is going to be a hit in America, while still being a Jackie Chan movie."

RB: So, now that you had explained your vision, what happened?
BR: He listened to me. He took me to the set of "Who Am I?" I met his father smoking a pipe. He drove me right back to the airport. He thought I was going to a hotel, but no, I was flying straight back. He was blown away that I was flying straight back, and that I had flown for 26 hours just to have lunch with him. A week later my agent called me and said, "Jackie Chan is going to do the movie!"

RB: You must have been ecstatic!
BR: That was like a game-changer for me. It changed my life. His decision to make the movie changed my life! A month later, Jackie called me and said, "I am coming to LA to meet you and Chris Tucker." When we met Chris Tucker, for twenty minutes he was saying, "I love you Jackie Chan, I love your movies man!" and was going on and on and on. Jackie was talking for about twenty minutes,

when Chris said to me, "Can I talk with you outside for a minute, Brett?" We were at William Morris' agency. I said, "Yes," Chris said, "Jackie Chan is not talking English! I don't understand one word he is saying. How we gonna do a movie with Jackie Chan if he don't speak English?" I said, "It's going to be fine Chris!" He replied, "You sure?" Of course I was! I said, "Yes, it will be fine!" Chris smiled. "Ok, I trust you, Brett." I went into the other room to see Jackie, and he said, "I like Chris, but I do not understand what he says!" I told him not to worry, and stressed that this was going to be brilliant! These guys didn't understand what they are saying to each other, but they loved each other!

RB: You're lucky - they had an instant liking for each other, despite the language barrier.

BR: They had chemistry. It wasn't something that I did, but something that happened organically. I said, "This is going to work!" And when they talked, whenever Chris could not understand what was coming out of Jackie's mouth, he would say, "Do you understand the words that are coming out of his mouth?!" to me. Those were the dynamics that made this relationship work, on and off screen. Timing was everything! And yes, the movie was so under the radar because nobody believed that a movie with a black guy and a Chinese guy would work. They were basically giving this HOT SHOT director a chance to make the movie that he thought was going to work, but to be honest, they never believed or thought that "Rush Hour" was going to work.

RB: So, obviously when Rush Hour was a success, you proved your doubters wrong.

BR: Yes! This is very important. Rush Hour was, at the time, the highest-grossing action comedy ever! It was bigger than Beverly Hills Cop, bigger than all the Lethal Weapons. The highest opening in the history of the studio. That was a huge, defining moment - not just for martial arts cinema, but for the fact that a black man and an Asian man were the stars. This opened my eyes. Someone could star in a movie and not have to be Tom Cruise, or Brad Pitt. Minority stars were making an impact. And that is why I believe that this is not just the first big martial arts movie, but a movie that opened the doors for underrepresented actors, which I think is more important - not just because the industry was open to it, but because it inspired the talented to go out and create. If you remember, Sammo Hung, who I am a huge fan of, got a TV series in the US (Martial Law)…

RB: I actually interviewed Sammo in the early nineties, and I believe that he thought that him crossing over was not going to happen, despite his worldwide fan base.

BR: That's right. I am not trying to take credit for this, but it was all about timing. It was something that was meant to be. Ultimately, would Jackie have crossed over without Rush Hour? Yes, he would. But the timing was right with me. Consider the fact that I grew up loving martial arts films, and was a huge fan of Jackie. I got my break with Money Talks, and showed

dedicated perseverance to fly 26 hours to have lunch with him in South Africa. Also consider the fact that his instincts didn't see me as some kind of hustler – he saw my passion and he knew that I was real. I said to him later, "Why did you choose me and my movie? Having been approached by every big director in Hollywood who

came to meet you and try to convince you to do a movie?" Jackie replied, "You were the first person, filmmaker, to tell me when you handed me the script that it was one of the worst scripts that you had ever read." He was totally surprised by that pitch and he said: "Every other person that sent him

a script, or met with him, or flew out to Hong Kong (and these were some big-name people) told him that their script was the best script in Hollywood." They must have thought that Jackie was some kind of idiot. Jackie Chan knew more about film-making than any of these guys. He had been making films since he was a young child. This is a guy that is Buster Keaton, Charlie Chaplin and Harold Lloyd rolled into one!

RB: Jackie Chan is, without a doubt, a genius when it comes to film-making.
BR: It's true. All he had to do was translate the script from English to Chinese and he could see straightaway that it was not good. But I told him, because I was just a kid, that the script sucked! But I also said that I was going to make it better, and that this was what I was going to do with it. He appreciated how real I was, and at that moment all the stars were aligned. I just happened to be a kid that grew up thousands of miles away from Hong Kong. I was living in Miami Beach. Nobody in my family was in the movie business, nobody in my family knew who Jackie Chan was, and there were absolutely no connections. People often think that I come from a rich family. The fact is that I knew nobody. I could have been anyone, because I knew nobody that worked in the movie business. What I had was a love and passion for Jackie Chan, Bruce Lee and martial arts films. And it was that passion and love for Hong Kong cinema that ultimately led me to that meeting with Jackie. I had a singular focus, and I knew what movie I wanted to make. To be honest, at that time I did not know how to make it, but I knew the movie that I wanted to make.

RB: Were there other movies being offered to you?
BR: Yes! I got offered 'hip hop' movies, but nothing that was going to be good. If I had just done those movies, it would probably have taken maybe ten, twenty years before I had a big hit. But, because Rush Hour was such a big hit, I got to write my own ticket. And because my

first movie, Money Talks, was a hit, this afforded me the opportunity to make whatever movie I wanted, and this meant I got to do Rush Hour next. That shot me so far ahead. And, of course, all Hollywood thinks about is MONEY $$$$. So, with the Rush Hour movie a hit, they thought, 'this kid knows what he is doing,' and that means you get left alone. Because when they looked at the statistics, there had never been a movie with an Asian and black guy that was a huge hit, and Rush Hour proved them wrong.

RB: What happened when you first started filming Rush Hour?

BR: When I started to film, Jackie and his team turned up - in fact you see Mars! a well known stuntman and regular face of the "Jackie Chan stunt team" in the opening scenes of Rush Hour, but sadly he could not come to LA. Now Jackie, when he is making a movie, will constantly watch the playback with his team. He gets his team, and they will count him out, shouting, "ONE, TWO, THREE, FOUR" in Chinese when filming. Then he will get those guys to tell him whether they got the shot! Meaning, on the playback, does it look like the punch connected? They have a lot of tricks specific to shooting a Hong Kong move. They speed up the film. They put powder on their feet.

RB: Yes, I am familiar with these tricks, even putting a sock or shoe in their hand to create a close-up shot if someone is being kicked in the face.

BR: Yep! They have all those tricks for fight scenes. But in America we do not have any of those tricks. It's completely different. But with Jackie's team they've always got his back, and are unaware of what I know. They know I know the script and the dialogue, but they assume that they will do the action. They have stunt directors and that's the way it is. During the first few weeks of filming, we had some disagreements, because I was challenging them. For instance, Jackie would say after a shot, "We got it, we got it," and I would say, "NO! We don't

have it!" Jackie would come over and I would say, "Look at the playback," and he would see it and go, "Good, got it," and I would say, "NO! Watch it again. That is good for Hong Kong, but not good for us!" Then he would be like, "OK! I do it again." After that kept happening, he stopped relying on his team so much. I mean, obviously they're his guys, but I was starting to almost become a part of the "Jackie Chan Stunt Team."

RB: That is some achievement, because Jackie knows what he wants and so does his crew, so he must have realised the importance of what you were saying.

BR: My goal was very specific. I never told Jackie to walk, throw a punch, go to the next guy, throw a kick, etc. What I did do, was have props over the pool table that you could break. I gave him pool balls that he could use, I gave him a stick that he could use. I tried to give him all the tools he needed, including a stool that he could also use. I gave him everything he could grab, knowing how Jackie works using any object close to him, to add to a fight scene. My attitude was: I do not care what happens, but you're going to start here and you're going to end up over there. I don't care what happens in-between. I don't care! The way my producer and the studio wanted me to shoot it was the way they shoot a fight sequence: you pre-choreograph it, and then you shoot everything in this direction, light it, and then you shoot it in the opposite direction. But Jackie does not film this way. Jackie figures this out in his head before we shoot. Sometimes, it led to problems. Jackie was going to fight some black guys. The guy swung his stick full force at Jackie's head. Now Jackie did not want to get hit, and it looked on the playback like he was ducking too soon. It was making Jackie frustrated, because he'd lost his rhythm with the stuntmen. It's like your wife - you know her so well, that if you dance with her, you know the way she moves, so you flow. But when you meet a girl at a nightclub and you dance with her for the first time, you're probably going to step on her toes! It feels awkward. Now the stunt guys, even though they were excellent stunt guys, didn't have that rhythm. So Jackie said, "Let me just use one of my Chinese guys like Andy Cheng." I am like, "Jackie you cannot do that! In Hong Kong you might be able to do that, but not here in America!" Now Jackie was stuck, and it might have been why, in the past, he might have been mis-quoted when he apparently said, "Oh, the process used in the US wasn't my process, but we got along fine. We became brothers."

RB: Can you explain the process?

BR: Sure. The filming process when shooting a fight scene was more complex. I would be getting messages from the studio saying, "Hey, Brett, this process is taking five times as long," even though they were not really bothering me. But we could still feel the pressure. The shooting, filming this angle, that angle, an angle back and forth as we were building the fight sequence – it was all pressured. We couldn't just pre-design it, because we did not know what the limitations were of the stuntmen. For the fight in the massage parlour in "Rush Hour 2," the same thing happened, even though this time he was fighting Asian guys. I decided to keep the girls in the fight, and you could see them reacting to this situation. Having Jackie fight one on one is easy. Once you incorporate Chris Tucker, who is not a fighter, and then you start incorporating extras, the scene starts to become more and more difficult. Jackie's frustration was more about the safety requirements. For example, when we were shooting the first movie in the LA Coliseum and Jackie was walking on the rafters, he went up there and shouted down, "Brett!" I looked up and shouted, "Jackie! Be careful!" He was jumping from beam to beam, and I am like, 'What the hell is going on?' The studio flipped out and had an emergency meeting, and I had to tell Jackie that he couldn't just go up there without having a safety harness. He said, "Oh come on!" I explained that we had insurance. Jackie being Jackie was doing risky stuff every day, like when he was filming in Hong Kong. The insurance company was then on the set every day. Watching Jackie pull off these huge stunts reminded me of when I was a kid, and me and my friends would go to a bridge and jump into the water. What I would do was get the dumbest kid to jump first, and if it looked safe, then we would jump in. What Jackie would do was get Andy Cheng to do something that was insane! Andy was fearless, and he wanted to prove to his big brother that he could do it. And if he did not get hurt, Andy would explain how he did it, and Jackie would do it. His method was to test ideas with human beings!

RB: So you were learning some valuable lessons?

BR: Yes. We flew to Hong Kong to film for the beginning of the movie, and I learnt two valuable lessons. If you remember, at the start of the movie there are two huge containers. These were to be pushed together by two tractors. The stunt was for Jackie to climb up the side of the container as they were being slowly pushed together, and I said to Jackie, "If you get stuck as they are pushing the containers together, they will still be pushing, and these are like ten tons each. The momentum means they cannot just stop!" Jackie said, "Ok," and he got two apple boxes and put them in-between the two containers, and said, "This will stop it." I looked and said, "I don't think so! APPLE BOXES?!" This was like tons of steel coming together! He smiled at me and said, "TRUST ME." He ran up the container, and when he reached the top, he slipped backwards with his legs still hooked to it. He fell backwards, and thank God he has strong stomach muscles, because he pulled himself up as the two containers slammed into each other. And you know what the two apple boxes did? They imploded into each other, crushed into dust.

RB: How did Jackie react to this near miss, which I am guessing was one of many in his career?

BR: He was literally shaking! I think he saw his life flash in front of him. So, imagine the last shot of the movie. Jackie gets KILLED! Imagine if I had killed Jackie Chan in my movie! I would have not only been hated, I would have been dead! I could imagine there being a hit on me. The headlines would have been: "Crazy Director Kills Jackie Chan." He did over 100 movies and nothing happened to him. He fell out of trees and survived all his crazy stunts. Jackie smiled, and said, "Ok, your way best!"

RB: The gods were smiling on you both that day (smiles)!

BR: True! The other thing that happened, and my second valuable lesson, was that we wanted to add some fight action in the convention centre at the end of the movie. And we did that thing where he had to catch all the priceless vases, and as he walked away, they fell. As an experiment, I printed two copies, as back then it was film. I struck two prints of each shot. I sent a copy to Jackie, who was in Hong Kong at the time, and I said to him, "I am going to let you cut the scene." I sent the other copy to my editor in LA. The editor sent it back and I did not look at it. Then, I sat there with Jackie. He was on the steenbeck, cut, cut cutting. It probably took my editor three days to put the scene together. Jackie, on the other hand, took only 4 hours. But - and here is the thing - he picked every single take that my editor picked, the exact same shot. Except, Jackie took out single frames.

RB: He took just single frames?

BR: Yes, he took just single frames to speed up the action. And I said, "Jackie, this should be taught in film school - the difference between the exact shots from an American movie and a Hong Kong movie. And, of course, we went with the American version. Not because the Hong Kong version was no good, but because you could see the speed up. For example, someone would throw a punch, and it would start here and end up there. They would lose all the frames in between, and subliminally US audiences were not used to that. Hong Kong audiences were. It's not just the subliminal fact, though, it's the suspension of belief. In an American movie, you had to see the connection in the punch. And for me, that is what I am most proud about. The movie takes the best of what Jackie does, but it does it in an American way. Believe me, I learnt stuff about action movies during the filming process that ensured that I never wanted to do another action movie! I did a heist movie, a romantic fantasy, a suspense movie, and a thriller with "Red Dragon." But, in my mind, I had done the best version of what I could do with an action movie, even though I had learnt some amazing tricks.

RB: What is Jackie like when he does get upset?

BR: There was one time when we were on the roof of a building, and Jackie and Chris had to look over the side of a roof. The way the producer decided to do this was to get a crane, put it on top of the roof, and tie the crane down. It took six hours to get each piece of the crane to the top. The crane was on a dolly, and so Jackie and Chris looked like they were looking over the top, while the crane with the camera took the shot. Jackie by now was so upset, and he shouted, "Brett, stop this bullshit!" I said, "What you talking about? We've got to secure the crane. I just can't have a camera operator hanging off the roof." Jackie looked at me and said,

"Watch." He got a rope, tied it around his waist, and got his Jackie Chan Stunt Team to hold the rope. He became like a human crane! He held the camera to his eyes, gave a signal and they slowly released him. It looked like Michael Jackson in that video for "Smooth Criminal." He leant forward at a 45-degree angle, took the shot, and then shouted, "OK!" They pulled him back, so it mimicked somebody looking over the edge. He turned round and said, "TWO MINUTES! You - SIX HOURS!" You could see his frustration, because in Hong Kong they did not have the insurance worries. There was very little safety, and if someone died, in most cases they would carry on, I am being facetious of course. Therefore, I always forgave Jackie if in an interview he said something negative about the production. Jackie had been making films longer than I had been alive. Jackie is the king of his own kingdom, and he was used to doing things his own way. And, of course, I understood that. To be honest, it wasn't a pleasant process, but in the end when he saw the movie, and how funny it was, even though the action was subpar to the action in his other movies, he understood that it was an A-list level movie for American audiences. The key thing is this: in films like "Police Story," or "Project A," or "Drunken Master 2," we saw amazing action that we weren't going to better. Our success was in developing a story that drove the movie forward. Rush Hour was a perfect East meets West movie. It was not by accident - it was specifically built that way. I was the guard and the protector of the Hollywood version, but I had such love and admiration of Hong Kong movies that I allowed as much of Jackie's Hong Kong style of filming as I could into Rush Hour, to create the perfect balance for audiences worldwide. This is what made Rush Hour a worldwide success.

RB: And finally, how was Jackie after watching the movie?

BR: Let me tell you, there was no one happier in the world than Jackie Chan after that screening!

RB: Brett, thank you for taking time out to chat. We could have talked a lot more, and maybe we will do another interview in another issue. But for now, thank you from me and all the readers of Eastern Heroes for taking time out to tell your story.

In special memory to Brett's beloved Grandma who sadly passed away shortly after this interview was conducted

JACKIE CHAN

By Michael Nesbitt

FAN CLUB 1989 - 1991

THE ULTIMATE IN HONG KONG MOVIES

Back in the 1980s and early 1990s, information on Hong Kong movies was hard to come by, in fact near on impossible. Living in Newcastle upon Tyne, made it even more difficult, because what little there was, i.e., Film shows, movie markets, Asian movie rental stores, were all either in or around London or the Midlands. So as a teenager, I had to rely on mail-order, specifically Shaolin Video, and the Jackie Chan Fan Club.

This was before the Internet was a thing, before Impact Movie Magazine had a monthly Asian action movie column, and before the influx of fanzines and other magazines. While snippets of information trickled through to England, most Asian VHS movies were sold on the black market, getting an original was like winning the lottery. So as a fan of Bruce Lee, Jackie Chan, Sammo Hung and Yuen Biao, I lapped up what little information there was out there, and purchased as much memorabilia as I could, with the little money that I had in my possession. However, in June of 1989, a bright light appeared on the horizon.

While reading an early 1988 issue of Combat martial arts magazine, I saw some news that captured my imagination. It stated in black and white, that coming soon to the UK, was the very first Jackie Chan Fan Club. The excitement I felt was unparalleled, and with the ever issue of Combat magazine that followed, I trawled through its pages in the hope that more information would appear. From around February 1989, adverts were starting to appear in martial arts magazines asking you to send a stamped addressed envelope for more information on the Jackie Chan Fan Club, so I of course sent off the SAE to Tempo House, which was situated at 15-17 Falcon Road in south-west London. Within weeks I received a membership application form with details stating that if you pay £10, you would become a lifetime member of the JCFC. It didn't take me long to fill

JACKIE CHAN IN WHEELS ON MEALS!

DONT MISS IT!

gives you a chance to buy six classic Jackie Chan movies, and a few martial arts movies released by Tamo Video. As a bonus, there is a 'Jackie Chan Promotional Sheet' which features 6 Jackie Chan movies.

Issue 2

The Issue 2 newsletter begins with an editorial from Rick Baker and Chris Alexis, where they talk about the delayed first issue, and movies such as Yuen Biao's Above the Law, and Jackie Chan's Police Story 2. They also discuss the upcoming Jackie Chan documentary, The Incredibly Strange Film Show with Jonathan Ross. Then we get to newsletter pages called 'A Small Selection of Jackie's Movie's which includes small write-ups of, Project A part 2, The Protector, Dragon Lord, The Young Master, Armour of God, Dragons Forever, Battle Creek Brawl and Winners and Sinners. Finally, we get the 'Jackie Chan Fact File' which gives information on Jackie's private life. This is followed in on the reverse of the page with two rare snaps of Jackie with his family and the Seven Little Fortunes, and 'Quiz No 2'.

Issue 3

Unlike the first two issues, which were newsletters, Issue 3 had been produced as an 8-page fanzine. Again we have an editorial from Rick and Chris, which started off with some good news and bad news. The bad news was that due to some unforeseen cost, the Fan Club

out the form and send it back with my subscription payment. All I had to do now, which was the hardest part, was to wait. When the day finally arrived, and the parcel was in my hands, I was brimming with excitement, to say that I was over the moon with what I received was an understatement.

Issue 1

The introductory package included the Jackie Chan Fan Club membership card, a sticker, a large poster of Jackie Chan depicting a behind the scene image for Project A, and several glossy newsletter-style pages. The first page was a print of a Jackie Chan drawing done by Dean Jones. The newsletter started off with an introduction of the people running the fan club, this is followed up with a 2 page, 4 sided, history of Jackie Chan movies. There is also a page called 'Film Review No 1' and reviews both First Mission and Winners and Sinners. The very first 'Jackie Chan Quiz' is included as is a 'Jackie Chan Merchandise List' which

(Videos of all your favourite Stars, Books, Photos, Posters)
T.V. monitors will be screening throughout the sale

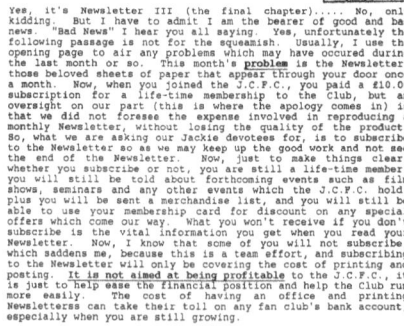

Star - Jackie', and reprints an article detailing the new Jackie Chan documentary, The Incredibly Strange Film Show, to be shown on Channel Four. This is followed up with 'Film Review No 2' which looks at Police Story Part 2 and Above the Law. Page 6, is 'Film News' which gives information about Sammo Hung's Pedicab Driver and The Dead and the Deadly. The next page is a 'Merchandise List' where you can purchase a VHS copy of Fearless Hyena Part 2, and the new Jackie Chan Poster. The back page has an advert for the Jackie Chan triple bill movie show at the Scala Cinema on Sunday, July the 23rd 1989, which would show the premiere of Police Story 2, plus Dragons Forever and Armour of God. As a bonus we get two full-colour glossy newsletter pages, the first is five never before seen photos from Jackie Chan's newest movie Miracles, and the second page is another 'A Small Selection of Jackie's Movie's sheet, which has write-ups of Police Story, My Lucky Stars and Project A.

Issue 4

Even though Issue 3 was officially the first issue of the JCFC fanzine, Issue 4 was the first issue to have a proper cover. The publication was still in black and white, but the added yellow to the cover made it stand out from anything that had come before. The cover artwork was done by Dean Jones who had already drawn a number of things for the JCFC in the past. The fanzine starts with 'Rick's Editorial', and an apology for the fanzine being late by a couple of months. He also mentions that there will be a questionnaire added to the fanzine for the new upcoming 'Bruce Lee and

could no longer run a subscription of a one-off payment of £10. You would still be a lifetime member, but you would only get details of films shows, events and merchandise lists sent through the door, now there would be an additional subscription charge to receive the monthly newsletter. With 450 members, the JCFC had to print off at least 1000 newsletters and to cover the costs the new subscription would now be £10 for 6 bi-monthly newsletters (one every two months). The good news was that they had the rights to show the premiere of Jackie Chan's Police Story 2 movie. It also gave details of the upcoming Bruce and Jackie Day, which was to be held at Leisure World in Birmingham on the 5th of August 1989. Page 4 of the newsletter was entitled 'Up-to-date Info on Your Favourite

Friends Network.' Then we move on to 'Summer Round-up and Current Events of 1989.' This included details on the Film Premiere of Police Story 2, the showing of Armour of God, Dragons Forever, and a 10-minute Jackie Chan promo film to promote 36 Crazy Fists. This section also includes details on the Bruce and Jackie Day in Birmingham, and The Martial Arts Movie Festival which was held on the 26/27 of August, and would feature special guest star, James Demile. A column called 'The Guide' was up next which would feature in several forthcoming issues, this issue spotlighting both Cynthia Rothrock and Yukari Oshima. 'Film Review' looked at Jackie Chan's upcoming movie Miracles. Then an article on 'Jackie Chan's Lost Classic' by John Brennan featured Hand of Death. This was followed up by an updated 'Jackie Chan Filmography 89'. The final article of the fanzine was 'The Ross Report' which took a look at the first episode of the Johnathan Ross TV series 'The Son of the Incredibly Strange Film Show,' which was a 45-minute special on Jackie Chan. The back cover had part 2 of the 'Jackie Chan Fact File.'

Issue 5

Unfortunately, there was no colour added to the cover of Issue 5, but it did have some rare actions shots of Jackie that had not been seen at the time. No editorial in this issue either, as it starts with, 'J.C. Manager, Willie Chan Speaks Out.' Willie talks about finishing up the filming of Jackie Chan's latest movie Miracles, the article had been taken from the Jackie Chan Hong Kong Fan Club. There is the 'Quiz', where you have to name the movie and the two stars pictured. Next up is 'Jackie Chan Fan Club Presents Martial Arts Triple Bill' which was a round-up of events from late 1989 to the latest film show in March 1990. The article goes into some detail about Cynthia Rothrock hosting the December 1989 film show, her latest

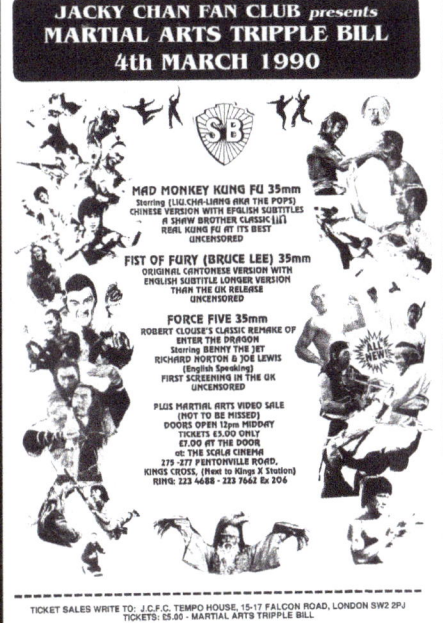

release in VHS, and her upcoming movie projects. Then it moves on to details about the upcoming film show triple bill which would feature the movies, Force Five, Mad Monkey Kung Fu, and the uncut version of Fist of Fury. A Jackie Chan merchandise list is next up, with some great Jackie Chan memorabilia up for grabs. Then there is the 'Video Action' article that takes a look at what's been happening in the movie world, including Antia Mui's Rouge, Sammo Hung's Painted Faces, and Yuen Biao's On the Run, amongst others. 'The Guide' returns in this issue, and features The Iceman Cometh, and an interesting look at Cynthia Khan. Up next is another merchandise advert, this time for a set of Jackie Chan audio cassettes, and 2 posters, and an advert for the upcoming martial arts movie event, which would sell loads of rare memorabilia, to be held at Cheung's Restaurant in New Oxford Street.

The back cover features rare photos of Jackie Chan on the set of Battle Creek Brawl.

Issue 6

Like in Issue 4, a bit of colour had been added to the cover, this time it was red, which made the cover stand out from all the previous issues, especially with the added bonus of an image of Jackie from the upcoming Armour of God 2 movie. For the first time, we have an index, copyright and intro. By now Chris Alexis and Rick had parted ways, and now it was only Rick that was in charge as editor and producer, with additional material from John Brennan and Bey Logan. The 'Intro' states for the first time that the team will be adding information on other famous Hong Kong action stars such as Yuen Biao, Sammo Hung and Dick Wei as well as many others. This would be the foreshadowing of the change in direction that was to come. Following the Index and Intro, we had a 'Picture Showcase' on Twinkle Twinkle Lucky Stars, with three rare shots from the movie. Pages 4-5 were the 'Club News 1990' Rick Bakers round-up of current events. Included in this was Rick's attempt to prise information from Bey Logan on Armour of God 2, which he managed successfully to gain a few rare images from the movie. We also get information about the upcoming triple bill movie event at the Scala, to be held on May the 27th. It would be UK premieres for all three movies, Aces Go Places starring Sam Hui and Karl Maka, Jet Lee's Kids from Shaolin and Sammo Hung and Maggie Cheung's Pedicab Driver. We then get the regular column 'The Guide' which includes two republished articles on Yuen Biao, one is on Peacock King 2, and the other is on Shanghai Shanghai. On page 7 we see a new feature called 'Shooting Star' by John Brennan, which looks in-depth at a specific Asian action star, this issue was Billy Chow. We then get another 'Video Action' article in which they take

a look at some femme fatales, including, Cynthia Rothrock, Cynthia Khan and Moon Lee. Then we get a splendid advert for the Scala Cinema triple Bill which was already mentioned. The next two pages are full-page adverts, the first being an advert for the James Demile seminar, which happened over 3 days. The second advert was for the new Chuck Norris UK Fan Club run by Maria Riley. Unfortunately, I don't think the fan club took off. On page 9 we have the 'Jackie Chan Quiz' and the final two pages are taken up with Rick's write-up of Cynthia Rothrock's first UK visit. The back page showcased three rare photos from Armour of God 2, which were talked about in the Intro.

Issue 7

One of the first action-packed covers to be released, featuring a host of Hong Kong stars, including, Jackie Chan, Sammo Hung, Yuen Biao, Andy Lau and Cynthia Khan. On the first page, we get a fantastic image of Dick Wei from Project A, the Index and Intro. This is followed up with 'Club News 1990' where Rick gives us a round-up of what's been happening in around the Jackie Chan Fan Club. With news on a possible Jean Claude Van Damme UK visit. We also get information on the Chuck Norris Fan Club, Jackie Chan and Olivier Grunner. In the 'Screen Scene' article, Rick chats about Teenage Mutant Ninja Turtles 2, Jet Lee's Dragon Fight and other titles. The 'Jackie Chan Quiz' is on page 6 and gives you an opportunity to win a copy of VPDs VHS released Police Story 2. John Brennan's 'Film Review' takes a look at two classics, The Prodigal Son and Warriors Two. And the 'Shooting Stars' section takes a close look at Hong Kong movie bad guy Dick Wei, including a filmography. An interesting article on 'Heroic Bloodshed' follows this, in which the team take a look at the gangster movie genre and the main actors to look out for. Bey Logan returns with his eagerly awaited article 'On Location AOG 2' which gives us the first insight on the making of Jackie Chan's Armour of God 2. Then we get a two-page article by Rick called 'Cindy in the UK' which gives some tantalising updates on Cynthia Rothrock and her upcoming movies. And finally, we get the 'Donnie Yen Profile' by Nick Gonet. The back page gives us a preview of Issue 8, which includes a chance to win a VHS copy of Above the Law.

Issue 8

Issue 8 becomes a milestone in action movie magazine history when it changes its name to 'Jackie Chan UK Fan Club incorporating Eastern Heroes'. Once again we get a two-tone cover, black and pink, with some great artwork by Al Davidson, depicting many faces from the action movie scene. Once

JACKIE CHAN FAN CLUB

presents

FIVE HOURS OF FURIOUS ACTION

SUNDAY
MAY 27TH

(DOORS OPEN 12.30PM)

UK Premiere

PEDICAB DRIVER

Samo Hungs Greatest Action Drama Since 'Eastern Condors' Best H.K. movie 1989 - not to be missed.

Kids From Shaolin

Eight times 'Wu Shu Champion' Jet Lee, demonstrates his true skill on screen, hailed as a martial arts genius by Jackie Chan.

Ace's Go Places

Takes of where Cannon Ball Run finished, with non stop crazy stunts, and a touch of the James Bond's - Chinese Comedy at its best.

DON'T FORGET 'BRING A WHISTLE'

3 filmS NOT TO BE MISSED
SCALA CINEMA

275-277 PENTONVILLE RD KINGS CROSS LONDON
(NEXT TO BRITISH RAIL AND TUBE STATION)

(MERCHANDISE STALL SELLING VIDEOS, T-SHIRTS, POSTERS)

---- CUT HERE ----

TICKETS £6.00 (J.C.F.C. MEMBERS)   £7.00 (NON-MEMBERS)   **£8.00 ON THE DOOR**

PLEASE SEND ME .... TICKETS

NAME ....

ADDRESS ....

MEMBERSHIP NO. ....   TOTAL £ ....

SEND TO: J.C.F.C. TEMPO HOUSE 15-17 FALCON RD LONDON SW11 2PJ   TEL. 223 4688

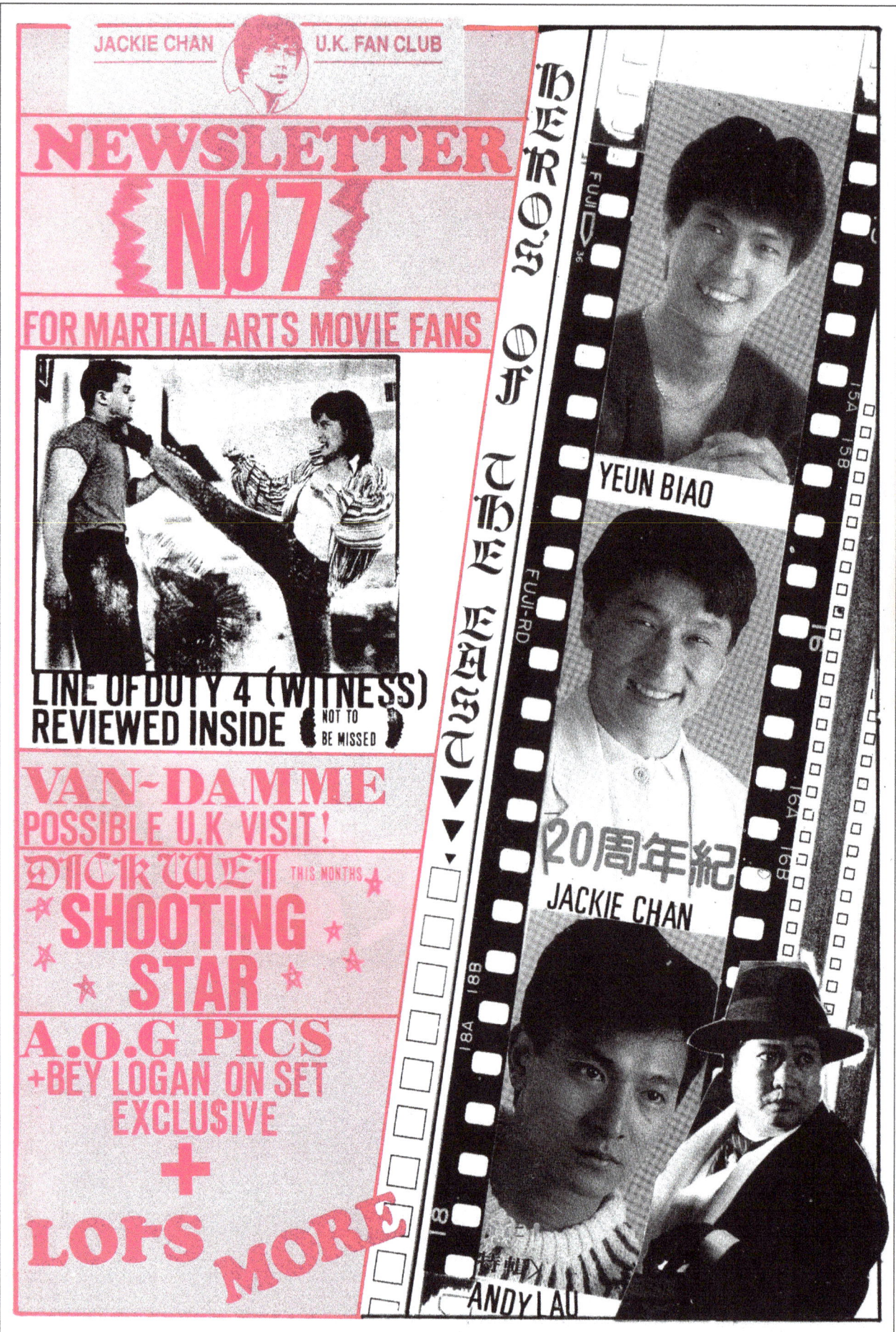

Houghton. The back page shows the wonderful movie poster artwork for the upcoming Jackie Chan movie Miracles.

Issue 9

On the cover of Issue 9, we get a wonderful piece of artwork of Donnie Yen, drawn by the legendary Al Davidson. On the first inside page, we get the customary index, with a great image from, In the Line of Duty 4. Rick Baker's 'Round-Up 1990' in which he takes a look at the popularity of Jackie Chan, Cynthia Rothrock and Donnie Yen. It also gives us some exclusive news on the upcoming visit of Donnie Yen to the UK, which was set for the 27th and 28th of October 1990. The 'Screen Scene Movie Round-Up' article includes info on Sammo Hung's Encounters of a Spooky Kind 2,

we open the pages, we get a glimpse at the index, with some rare photos of Jackie Chan. 'Round-Up 1990' where we get the latest info on Jackie Chan's Miracles, and the upcoming movie triple bill at the Scala Cinema, which was Jet Lee's Dragon Fight, Jackie Chan's Wheels on Meals and the Venoms Shaolin Daredevils. The show was scheduled for the 19th of August 1990. The 'Screen Scene Movie Round-Up' article takes a look at Line of Duty 5, Tiger Cage 2 as well as many others. 'Shooting Stars' highlights the brit martial arts action star Mark Houghton, while the 'Twins of Kung Fu' article takes a look at Sammo Hung and Leung Kar Yan. A new section called 'Cult Movie of the 90s' goes in-depth into Sammo's Skinny Tiger Fatty Dragon, in which he co-stars with the legendary Karl Maka. This is followed up by an article on the director Tsui Hark, written by Peter Smith. The 'Quiz' is up next, with a chance to win a copy of the newly released Above the Law, starring Yuen Biao and Cynthia Rothrock. The Video was supplied by Cynthia herself and was signed. In the regular Cynthia Rothrock column, the team take a close look at Cynthia's newest movie City Cops, in which she takes on Mark

Chow Yun Fat's The Killer, and Casino Raiders 2. Next up we have a two-page 'Profile on Hwang Jang-Lee' by John Brennan, and on pages eight and nine there is a 'Coming Soon Pics and Story from Miracles'. The 'Shooting Stars' column has Yukari Oshima profiled, and Bey Logan profiles 'Donnie Yen - The Dragon Discovered'. Page 14 has a full-page advert for the Jackie Chan Fan Club, with the new subscription charges, which were, £12.50 for 6 bi-monthly issues or £6.50 for half a year subscription of 3 issues. The final article in this issue is the 'Cult Movie of the 90s' which takes a look at John Woo's The Killer. The back cover shows three exclusive photos from the set of Jackie Chan's Armour of God 2: Project Eagle.

Issue 10

Issue 10 was no longer a fanzine, now it had become a high quality feel magazine and had a great behind the scenes photo of Jackie Chan on the set of Armour of God 2: Project Eagle.

On the contents page, there was now an 'Editor's Note', which informed readers that there was a change of address, which was a P.O. Box in South East London. Rick Baker's 'Round-Up 1990/91' looked at the best releases of 1990, and the BBC 2 Chinese Ghost Story Season, showed classics such as Mr Vampire, Spooky Encounters and Zu Warriors for the first time on British TV. It also included 'Rick Bakers Awards for 1990' the winners being: Best Newcomer: Donnie Yen. Best Director: John Woo. Best Western Martial Artist: Jean Claude Van Damme. Best Achievement of the Decade: Jackie Chan. And Best Film of 1990: The Killer. Next up was an article on the 'Standard Film Festival' in which they acknowledged Hong Kong movies for the first time. A new regular column was on pages six and seven, 'Hollywood East' which reported what was hot and what was not around the globe. It featured stars such as Maggie Cheung, Andy Lau, Yuen Biao and Joyce Godenzi. The next four pages were dedicated to Armour of God 2, now renamed Project Eagle, starting with 'Desert Melting Point', which detailed the difficulties of making the movie, with

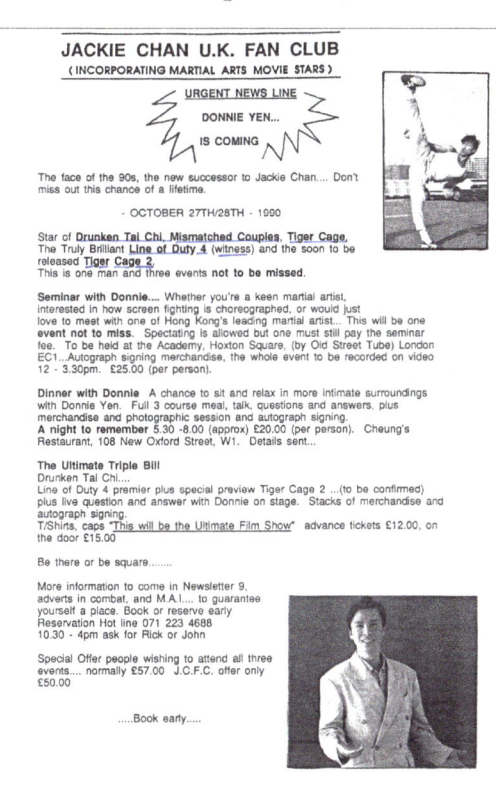

many unseen photos from the set. This was followed up with 'Insight into Project Eagle' which shared some fascinating information about the movie and cast. The back cover shared some amazing photos of Gordon Liu's visit to the UK with Mark Houghton, and information on the next issue.

Issue 11

This bumper issue with 24 pages was to be the last issue that used the Jackie Chan Fan Club title. The glossy cover had a great black and white image of Chow Yun Fat from The Killer. Right after the contents page, we have the 'Editors Round-Up' in which Rick Baker shared the latest news, including, Loren Avedon's UK visit for Clash of the Titans event on May 4th 1991. Operation Condor, (Previously named Armour of God 2) had finally hit the movie theatres. The movie went straight to the No 1 spot with Chow Yun Fat's Once a Thief and Sammo Hung's Gambling Ghost coming in close behind. John Brennan picks his best of 1990s

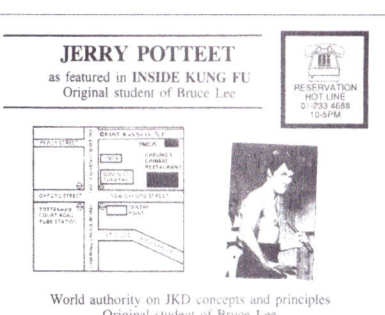

RETURN OF THE DRAGONS
BRUCE LEE & JACKIE CHAN ROADSHOW

XMAS SHOW

ADMISSION £1

DEC 16th, (Saturday)
Doors open 12-6pm

KICK FIT GYM, LEISURE WORLD BIRMINGHAM
3rd Floor, 55 Station Street, Birmingham BJ 4DY
RARE BRUCE VIDEOS   JACKY AND OTHERS
LIVE DEMOS (VIDEO SHOW)   POSTERS AND LOTS OF GOODIES

------- CUT HERE -------

We/I am interested in the attending the Bruce & Jackie Roadshow, also information regarding the new Bruce Lee fan club "Bruce Lee & Friends"

Please tick box   ☐ Tickets to Bruce & Jackie Roadshow
                   ☐ I would like to be a member of Bruce Lee & Friends

Could you please send me further details.

Name ....
Address ....
.... Postcode ....

J.C.F.C.
Tempo House
15-17 Falcon Road
London SW11 2P5
01-223 4688
for details

JCFC presents
CYNTHIA ROTHROCK
The Queen of Kung Fu
2nd December   YWCA   1pm - 3pm
YWCA Great Russell Street (see map at front)

Star of
- ABOVE THE LAW
- BLONDE FURY
- SHANGHAI EXPRESS
- CHINA O'BRIEN
- YES MADAM
- INSPECTOR WEARS A SKIRT

Your chance to train with the Queen of Kung Fu (Movie Star)
2nd December learning power kicking, stretching techniques,
Wu-Shu also Eagel Claw

1pm - 3pm   Cost £20   Limited Tickets
Venue: YWCA, Great Russell Street (see map at front)

CYNTHIA ROTHROCK FAN CLUB (formed)
Membership £10
Newsletter
Videos/Training tape
Signed photos
Posters
Filmography
and lots more
223 4688 for further details

DINNER
with the Queen of Kung Fu
CYNTHIA ROTHROCK
A 3 course meal
at Cheung's Restaurant
Informal chat/question/answer
Advice on how to break into
the Hong Kong film industry
Tips on preparation work needed
What to look for
Personalised photo session
Merchandise available
Price £15   2nd Dec 1989
Venue: Cheung's (see map at front)

SUN DEC 16 DOORS OPEN 12 NOON

XMAS SHOW
THIS IS A MARTIAL CLUB PRESENTATION
CYNTHIA ROTHROCK FILM SHOW

DOUBLE BILL

CITY COPS (PREMIER, SUBTITLED) 35MM
STARRING THE DEADLY DUO CYNTHIA ROTHROCK AND MARK HOUGHTON

CODE OF FORTUNE (PREMIER, SUBTITLED) 35MM
SAMO HUNG (NEW)

**SPECIAL GUEST FOR THE DAY
CYNTHIA ROTHROCK IN PERSON**
NOT TO BE MISSED
HAVE YOUR PHOTOS TAKEN WITH CHINA O'BRIEN AND AUTOGRAPHS
MERCHANDISE STALL, LATEST MODERN DAY & TRADITIONAL MOVIES IMPORTED
FROM THE FAR EAST
RIO CINEMA, 107 KINGSLAND HIGH STREET, E8 2PB
TRAVEL: STATION NEAREST TO VENUE, DALSTON KINGSLAND STATION (NET. SOUTH EAST), LIVERPOOL ST., BUSES 149, 243, 67, KINGS X 38 OR 30 TO DALSTON JUNCTION

TICKETS £8 IN ADVANCE, £10 AT THE DOOR

ROTHROCK SEMINAR
TO BE HELD AT
SATURDAY 15TH DECEMBER 3-5PM £25

CENTRAL CLUB (YWCA)
16-22 GREAT RUSSELL ST.
LONDON WC1
OFF TOTTENHAM COURT ROAD
LIMITED PLACES
DEFEND YOURSELF, 10 MASTER MOVES
CYNTHIA'S LATEST SELF DEFENCE VIDEO WITH
24 PAGE INSTRUCTION MANUAL
SIGNED BY CYNTHIA ON THE SPOT

XMAS DINNER
WITH CYNTHIA ROTHROCK

FIGHT TO WIN SNEAK PREVIEW
SOON TO BE RELEASED ON VIDEO

CHEUNG'S CHINESE RESTAURANT
108 NEW OXFORD STREET, LONDON WC1
LIMITED PLACES
PRICE £25 PER HEAD
INCLUDES 3 COURSE MEAL AND DRINKS
PLUS VIDEO SHOW, EXCERPT FROM HER LATEST MOVIE
SOON TO BE RELEASED IN UK ON VIDEO, 'FIGHT TO WIN' SNEAK PREVIEW

3 COURSE MEAL AND DRINKS ONLY £25

SATURDAY 15TH DECEMBER, RESERVATION 071-738 2506

FOR ALL CYNTHIA ROTHROCK EVENTS
CONTACT 'KUNG FU' CHRIS OR JASON 'BEARDY JNR.' (STAR OF CH 4'S THE WORD)
HOTLINE 071-738 2506/3, 223 8049
24HR 0860 576186 (COSMIC)

WE ARE THE PEOPLE WHO MAKE THINGS HAPPEN

awards in an article entitled 'Best of the Best 1990'. This is followed up with 'The Master's Tour' detailing Gordon Liu's visit to the UK with Mark Houghton. Another three-page article is next 'The Prodigal Son of Golden Harvest' this time detailing the life and career of Yuen Biao. Then there's a full-page advert for the star of No Retreat no Surrender 2, Loren Avedon's visit to the UK. The 'Hollywood East' column looks as Chow Yun Fat, God of Gamblers, Jackie Chan and Paper Marriage. 'Look Back in Anger' is the first of a three-part article by Rick Baker looking at the movies and characters that make up the Heroic Bloodshed movie genre. On page 17 we find the 'Quiz', with a chance to win Jackie Chan and Donnie Yen T-shirts. In Bey Logan's article, 'A Run in the Tights: Pantyhose Hero' he delves deep into this underrated Sammo Hung classic movie. In the final article of the issue, 'She's Got the Power' Bey Logan takes a close look at powerhouse femme fatale, Michiko Nishiwaki. The back cover shows us the original poster for Joyce Gondenzi's Lethal Lady (She Shoots Straight).

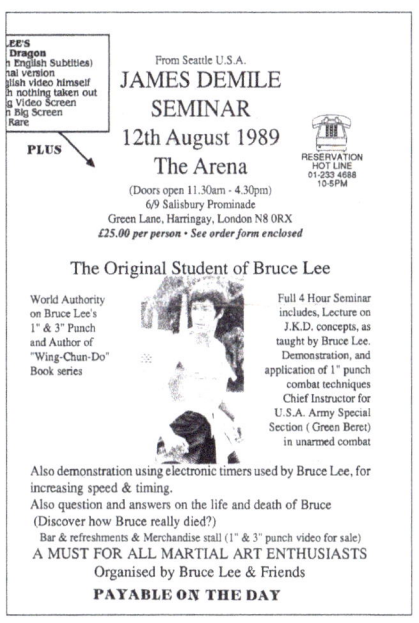

This was the last time the Jackie Chan Fan Club released a magazine. From issue 12 onwards the magazine morphed completely into Eastern Heroes and would change the face of action movie magazines forever. Without the Jackie Chan Fan Club newsletters, fanzines, magazines, roadshows, movie screenings and guest stars, the Hong Kong action movie scene of the late 1980s and early 1990s would have not been as successful in the UK. For many of the fans of the genre, the Jackie

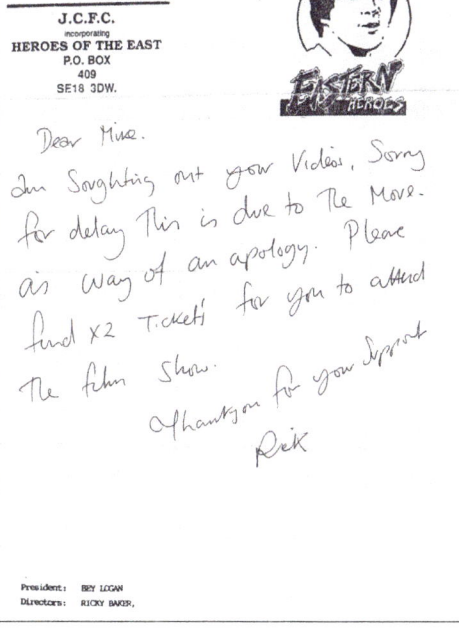

Chan Fan Club publications and events were their gradual introduction into the world of Asian action movies and its stars and paved the way for the likes of Impact Movie Magazine, and all the Asian Movies that would eventually be released in Britain on VHS, DVD and Blue-ray.

"THE EAGLE HAS LANDED"

JACKIE CHAN MERCHANDISE—LIST

POSTER PACKAGE

rolled NO creasing (black & white)

- THE BIG BRAWL - Championship Fight
- New Fist of Fury / Mad Monkey Kung Fu / Unbeatable Dragon (The Jackie Chan Fan Club presents, On 23rd of April At the Scala Cinema, 275-277 Pentonville Rd, Kings Cross, London. Doors open 12.30pm. Admission £6.00, J.C.F.C. members £5.00) (full colour)

special Offer all 3 for £2.50 (75p P&P)

6 - J.C stickers yellow with black jc motif ONLY £1.00

new martial arts movie trailers

over 100 MINS of non stop action £15.00 £1.50 P+P
INCLUDES: Shanghai Shanghai, Rush, Eastern Condors, Pedicab Driver, Miracles, K.ng of Duty III, Magic Crystal, Eyes of the Dragon, Shanghai Express, Absent the Law, + Many More.

FAX-LINE
Tel: 01-223 4688
Fax: 01-223 7116

JACKIE CHAN U.K. FAN CLUB
TEMPO HOUSE
15-17 FALCON ROAD
LONDON SW11 2PJ

JACKIE CHAN MERCHANDISE—LIST

BRUCE LEE POSTER SELECTION
(following Posters are large bedroom size Posters) £3.95 + 50p P & P

- B.L. 1) Nuchaku Pose Fist of Fury
- B.L. 2) Bruce 1/2 Body Pose Coliseum W.O.D.
- B.L. 3) Enter the Dragon Fighting Pose
- B.L. 4) Enter the Dragon Mirror Pose and Multi B/W Shots Fist of Fury
- B.L. 5) Enter the Dragon Full Frontal
- D.L. 6) Game of Death 1/2 Body Shot in Fighting Pose

DEEP COLOUR JAPANESE LAMINATED POSTERS (A2 SIZE)
(Limited amounts subject to availability) £4.00 each, .50p P & P

- B.L. 7) Multi Shot with Large Front Pose 'Smiling' Enter the Dragon.
- B.L. 8) Fighting Sequence 'Fist of Fury' in Japanese 'Dojo'.
- B.L. 9) Full body shot, in pose with Enter' Bruce posing in Hall of Mirrors.
- B.L. 10) 1/2 body shot, fighting pose 'Enter'.
- B.L. 11) Enter the Dragon Full Body Shot. From Hall of Mirrors, Enter the Dragon.

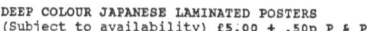

JACKIE CHAN POSTERS SELECTION
(Following Posters are large bedroom size) £3.95 + .50p P & P

- J.C. 1) Jackie in Training, with cups and rings on Arm, in horse stance, from Drunken Master.
- J.C. 2) Jackie in publicity shot in tracksuit, Posing in fighting stance with wooden staff.

DEEP COLOUR JAPANESE LAMINATED POSTERS
(Subject to availability) £5.00 + .50p P & P

- J.C. 3) Half body shot (no shirt) in martial art stance.
- J.C. 4) Multi shot from The Protector
- J.C. 5) Multi shot (7 pictures) of Jackie in fighting pose.

Incredibly stange Picture show
'documentry on jacky chan – as screened on channel 4' £9.99 + 75p P+P

Please write your order on seperate Paper

MERCHANDISE LIST

JACKIE PORTRAIT BY DEAN JONES FROM ISSUE NO. 7	£1.00 EACH
NEWSLETTER BACK ISSUES 1, 2, 3 (ONLY ONE PER PERSON) INCLUDING FOLDER	£8.00 PER SET
BIG BRAWL POSTER (SPECIAL OFFER) WERE £2.95 EACH SCALA CINEMA POSTER (SPECIAL OFFER) NOW ONLY	£1.50 EACH
J.C. FOLDER (SPECIAL OFFER) WAS £2.95 NOW (ONLY ONE PER PERSON)	£2.00
J.C. NEWSLETTER NO. 4 (16 PAGE B/W INCL. MIRACLE REVIEW/HAND OF DEATH)	£2.50
AUDIO SOUNDTRACKS - YOUNG MASTER	£5.00
PROTECTOR	£5.00
BIG BRAWL	£5.00
ARMOUR OF GOD	£5.00
SPECIAL XMAS OFFER ALL FOUR FOR	£18.00
THE PROTECTOR - LIMITED POSTER, FULL COLOUR A2. PICTURE SHOWS MULTIPLE SHOTS	£2.50
ARMOUR OF GOD - LIMITED POSTER, FULL COLOUR A2. JACKIE WITH CROSSBOW	£2.50
FEARLESS HYENA PART II (ENGLISH)	£19.95
SPIRITUAL KUNG FU	£19.95
CHAN BEHIND THE SCENES VIDEO DOCUMENTARY (60 MINS APPROX) 1 HOUR	£20.00
HAND OF DEATH VIDEO - ENGLISH VERSION	£25.00
NEW POSTER, A3 COLOUR, MIRACLE	£5.00
BRUCE LEE TRANSFERS - SET OF 6 DIFFERENT ITEMS, FULL SIZE FOR T/SHIRTS. LIMITED.	£4.95 PER SET

WE ALSO HAVE A RANGE OF STILLS, FULL COLOUR, LAMINATED, A3 SIZE. UNFORTUNATELY, WE DO NOT HAVE SPACE TO SHOW YOU THE PICTURES BUT A DESCRIPTION IS OFFERED TO HELP YOU CHOOSE. STILLS ARE LIMITED AND COST £1.50 EACH. ALL STILLS ARE EXCEPTIONALLY RARE.

- PAINTED FACES - STILL SHOWS POSTER ADVERTISEMENT
- EASTERN CONDORS - STILL SHOWS POSTER ADVERTISEMENT
- HALF A LOAF OF KUNG FU - MULTI SHOTS FROM MOVIE
- REVENGE OF DRUNKEN MASTER - POSTER ADVERT, JACKIE WITH VASE
- REVENGE OF DRUNKEN MASTER - SYNOPSIS + PHOTOS
- FILM SHOW POSTER, NOV 27TH 1988. ARTWORK BY DEAN JONES. SUPERB COLOUR ILLUSTRATION - EASTERN CONDORS, PROJECT A II, DRAGONS FOREVER.
- THE PROTECTOR - AMERICAN POSTER WITH PHOTOGRAPHIC PICTURES
- SNAKE IN EAGLES SHADOW - JACKIE
- SNAKE IN EAGLES SHADOW - JACKIE IN TRAINING
- SNAKE IN EAGLES SHADOW - JACKIE IN BATTLE
- DRAGON LORD - JACKIE CLIMBING HUMAN PYRAMID
- JACKIE 1 - A2 FULL COLOUR POSTER - JACKIE IN HALF BODY SHOT IN KUNG FU POSE - £5.00
- JACKIE 2 - A2 FULL COLOUR POSTER - JACKIE IN SECOND HALF BODY SHOT - £5.00

PLEASE ALLOW 28 DAYS WHEN ORDERING, AS IF A PRODUCT SELLS OUT, WE DO TRY TO RE-ORDER SO AS NOT TO DISAPPOINT.

PLEASE ADD 75P POSTAGE AND PACKING TO ALL ORDERS FOR STILLS AND AUDIO CASSETTES, £1.00 PER VIDEO. POSTERS A2 SIZE FREE P+P.

NAME .... ADDRESS ....
MEMBERSHIP NO. ....
DATE ORDERED ....

PLEASE SEND ORDERS TO:- J.C.F.C., MAIL ORDER, 15-17 FALCON RD., LONDON, SW11 2JP.

order for christmas

J.C.F.C. MERCHANDISE LIST "AUTUMN"

DRAGONS FOREVER T/SHIRT (Exclusive J.C.F.C. Design)
White 100% cotton T/Shirt comes emblazoned with the famous trio 'Jackie Chan, Yuen Biao, Samo Hung in full colour on white background with the logo 'Dragons Forever' as they are referred to .... limited stock makes this a genuine collectors piece ... sizes are M, L, XL ..... (please state when ordering).
Cost is £6.95 + 50p P & P ......
'Design shown opposite'.

'ARMOUR OF GOD'. Full super gloss poster 'Picture' depicts Jackie with crossbow (size A3). Cost £2.95

'PROTECTOR POSTER' super high gloss, multi-picture shot (size A3). Cost £2.95

(Both Posters £5.00....75p P & P)

NEWSLETTER BACK ISSUES.

ISSUE NO. 4 Miracle Review ... Jackie Pics' £2.50

ISSUE NO. 5 Willy Chan speaks out, more Jackie Pics £2.50

ISSUE NO. 6 Jackie shaping up for A.O.G.2., Cynthia Rothrock column, shooting star 'Billy Chow' £2.50

ISSUE NO. 7 New Look Magazine, incorporates Eastern Heros Bye Coyan 'Exclusive' A.O.G.2. report. Shooting Star 'Dick Wei' Cynthia Rothrock pictures, film reviews. £2.50

ISSUE NO. 8 'Samo Hung Report' shooting star 'Mark Houghton' 'Thin Tiger Fat Tiger' exclusive review ... Cynthia Rothrock in 'City Cops' ... £2.50

ISSUE NO. 9 Donnie Yen Special, includes interview with Donnie from H.K. Shooting Star Yukuri Osnima, Miracle Pic's and story. Whang Jan Lee (super kicker) profile. £2.50

ANY '3' 'SPECIAL OFFER' £6.00 FREE P & P...

AUDIO CASSETTES (SOUNDTRACKS ONLY)

Armour of God	£4.00	The Protector	£4.00
Young Master	£4.00	The Big Brawl...	£4.00

Battle Creek Brawl

Kung-Fu, Roller Skates and the Great Depression – Jackie Chan's Fabulous First Stab at America!

By Jason McNeil

In the early 1980s, Jackie Chan was the World Cup Soccer of movie stars: beloved and watched by millions of devoted fans around the world, and no one in America seemed to notice, aside from the fact the he was "that Japanese guy from The Cannonball Run, right?" But, like World Cup, the dream of cracking the mighty American Market drew Jackie back again and again, like so many Peles and David Beckams before and after him. Unfortunately, it wasn't until the mid-90s that Chan finally conquered the American box office with a savvy combination of re-releases (Rumble in the Bronx), an inspired PR blitz ("He does his own stunts!") and finally settling into the breakthrough winning formula of pairing him in buddy cop style action films where he could simultaneously show off his karate chops and his comedy chops that Jackie Chan's star finally shone bright amongst the Stars and Stripes.

During the fifteen years before that, though, Jackie took a few mostly-unsuccessful stabs at the American market that left a truly mixed bag for fans of kung-fu film fighting. From The Protector (1985) to memorable supporting roles in The Cannonball Run (1981) and The Cannonball Run 2 (1984) to – and here we come to the crux of the lesson – the absolutely batshit, bombastic and brilliant bouillabaisse that is 1980's Battle Creek Brawl! It was a plan so simple, it had to work!

In East Asia and around the world, Jackie Chan was the biggest kung-fu star since Bruce Lee, so what better way to break Jackie in America than to just follow the Bruce Lee path to superstardom, right? Bruce's death in 1971, just before the release of Enter the Dragon, left a hole in action cinema that everyone from David Carradine to Jim Kelly to Joe Lewis had been desperately trying to fill. For someone who walked around in size 7 sneakers1, The Little Dragon's shoes had, thus far, proven waaaay too big to fill. So – shit! - let's just give Jackie Chan his own Enter the Dragon!2 Its bound to work, right? The pitch meeting, as I imagine it went: "OK, first things first. We hire Robert Clouse, the Director of Enter the Dragon. Also, we'll get Fred Weintraub, who was the Producer of Enter the Dragon. And the Director and Producer of Enter the Dragon will get together and come up with a story about... oh, I don't know... a kung-fu guy who is recruited to fight in a big martial arts tournament. Just like in Enter the Dragon! And we'll get Pat Johnson, who played a mob thug in Enter the Dragon to play a mob thug in this one, too. Oh, and he'll be the stunt coordinator!" Fat studio guys in wide lapelled disco suits and loud ties are nodding along, smoking Freudianly large cigars. "And also there will be ROLLER SKATING, and lots of professional wrestlers, and the big scary Bolo-esque fighter likes to KISS GUYS after he beats them up – its kind

of his thing – and, also, its set in Texas, during the Great Depression. Did I mention there's roller skating? ROLLER SKATING WITH FIRE HOSES!"

Yes, Battle Creek Brawl wears its Enter the Dragon pedigree on its sleeve like one of Will Smith's kids trying to get a record contract, but it brings to bear more unexpected action

and excitement than most any tournament movie you'll ever see! Sure, the Tournament Movie is a staple of martial arts cinema, but Battle Creek Brawl sets itself apart both by

sheer Young Jackie Chan badassery AND the inclusion of a number of story elements I PROMISE YOU you will never see potboiled and blended together in the same film anywhere else! There's never a dull moment, here – but don't just take my word for it. Let's give it a quick rundown: Jackie play Jerry Kwan, the second son of a stern Chinese father who is constantly exhorting him not to fight and berating him for wasting his time

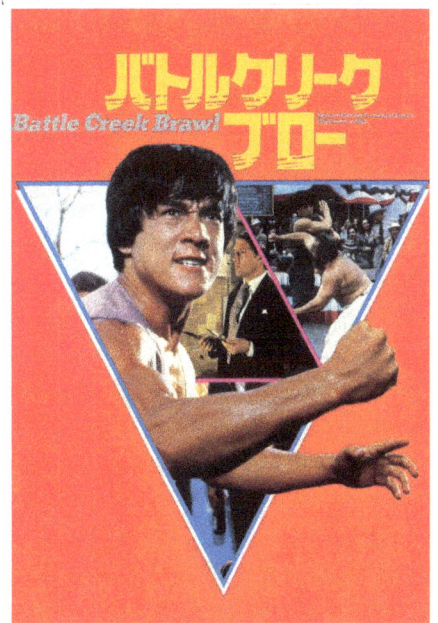

with kung-fu instead of becoming a doctor, like his older brother. (I am told that "Why aren't you a doctor like your brother?" is an integral part of growing up Chinese.) Jerry, however, is only interested in two things: his pretty blonde girlfriend, Nancy, and learning kung-fu from his Uncle Herbert, a chiropractor with a fondness for fat women.

We'll come back to the chubby-chasing kung-fu chiropractor in a moment, but let's pause first and marvel at the perfection that is Kristine DeBell. A beautiful blonde actress who had a decent run in the 80s, DeBell was most famous (or, perhaps, infamous) around this time as the titular star of the 1976 X-Rated musical porno comedy (read that again) Alice in Wonderland, in which Alice falls down the rabbit hole then wanders from costumed singing sex scene to costumed singing sex scene, often joining in the singing, and occasionally joining in the sex.3 In Battle Creek Brawl, she is absolutely delightful as Jerry's spunky, "I do what I want, even if its dating a Chinese guy in the 1930s" girlfriend, and really brings a nice presence to the film. She and Jackie have a playful chemistry, and you totally buy them as a young, kinda weird couple in love.

Back to Uncle Pork Pounder. When he's not cracking backs, he's blasting fat. For no discernible reason – besides the fact that its just amazing – not once, not twice but THRICE over the course of the film do we see Uncle Herbert taking a break between his "Cruel Tutelage" training sessions to slip off and feed the banana to a series of chunky monkeys. Besides being a badass kung-fu master, Uncle Herbert is a PLAYA and, mind you, he was liking all these big butts a full dozen years before Sir Mix-A-Lot! #Respect

OK, the plot: The linear version is that Jerry's father, who owns a restaurant, is being shaken down by the Chicago mob. Jerry kung-fus some of the collection mooks in the alley behind the restaurant, including Pat Johnson, basically reprising his role from Enter the Dragon, and Lenny Montana, who played Luca Brassi in The Godfather, basically reprising his role as Luca Brassi, though he's referred to at different times as Johnny, Angel and Johnny Angel. Whatevs. Hearing of Jerry's fighting prowess, Mob Boss Dominici (Jose Ferrer) decides, as one does when one is a 1930s Chicago Mob Boss, that young Jerry sounds like the perfect guy to be his entry in the Battle Creek Brawl, a bare-knuckle, anything goes fighting competition in Texas that is totally illegal yet somehow everyone knows about and uniformed cops turn out to watch. Jerry doesn't want to fight, so Boss Dominici has him kidnapped and threatened and cajoled and, ultimately, tells him about the $15,000 first prize4, which had to sound pretty sweet in the middle of The Great Depression, so Jerry agrees to be Dominici's fighter in the tournament. And they go to Texas and fight. You've seen this all before, right? Wrong. I won't go into too much detail, because of

Jackie Chan in Battle Creek Brawl

spoilers, but here's a breakdown of all the bells and whistles and totally batshit extras you get at no additional charge with your Battle Creek Brawl viewing experience:

• Presumably because Jackie Chan's English was somewhat limited at the time, and also presumably because Jackie wanted to show off his unique style of "kung-fu meets Keystone Cops slapstick" physical skills, there is far less standing around and chatting than one would expect. Exposition shmexposition! When we are introduced to Jerry and Nancy, she is patiently waiting for him in a car, shouting for him not to wear himself out, while Our Hero does a completely gratuitous but impressive high bar routine, thirty feet over a rusty old bridge! There are multiple "Rocky training montage" style sequences. Don't forget – this was Jackie trying to show off to a brand new audience, so there's some really cool stuff in there!

• For a fun night out, Jerry and Nancy enter a Full Contact, Indoor/Outdoor Roller Derby, where the skaters are repeatedly blasted with a high-pressure fire hose as they try to struggle up a concrete ramp! There is no discernible plot reason for any of this, but it is AWESOME! More than that – its AWESOME ON WHEELS!

• Though there are some scenes where Jackie looks to have brought in guys who more suit his fighting style, including his "audition" fight for Boss Dominici on an amphitheater stage that is sort of a "Greatest Hits" version of the horse bench fight from Drunken Master, the majority of the action – and the entirety of the tournament – is Jackie adapting his style to fighting Hollywood guys, real karate guys (including Pat Johnson, whom Jackie defeats partially by grabbing a big handful of one of Pat's ass cheeks and squeezing until the mook falls down) and, at the tournament, a bevy of what are CLEARLY 1970s professional wrestlers, doing their 1970s professional wrestler thing!

JACKIE CHAN
BATTLE CREEK BRAWL

Sure, we can all agree that Bloodsport is a classic of the genre, but can you imagine Van Damme using civilians for cover while Bolo picks up spectators and throws them at him? You bet your ass you can't!

What Battle Creek Brawl offers up is a very unique film that exists at the overlap between the Venn Diagrams of Enter the Dragon and Heaven's Gate. It shouldn't work, but it does, and there is nothing else like it, anywhere. A totally unique spin on the tropes of the tournament movie and absolutely dripping with its own brand of unvarnished badassery. Unfortunately at the time, it didn't click with cinema-goers.

In his autobiography, I Am Jackie Chan, the Chan Man recalls that he thought Director Robert Clouse didn't "get" what he was all about, and the movie didn't work because he wasn't allowed to fully strut his stuff in all its Jackie Chan glory. Recalling one scene where he wanted to flip out of a car, Clouse wanted him to just get out and walk like a normal human getting out of a car, and the star admonished him "No one will pay to see Jackie Chan walk!" Unfortunately, Battle Creek Brawl's failure to do Star Wars numbers at the box office isn't quite as simple as Jackie makes it out to be. It was 1980, for Sly's sake!

In the Big Guns, Big Pecs Era of Stallone

THE BIG BRAWL

and Arnold, America just wasn't feeling a "funny guy" action hero performing slapstick kung-fu - no matter how brilliantly done - that was equal parts Buster Keaton and Chinese Opera. What should've been Jackie Chan's place in the spotlight was usurped in short order by "The Muscles from Brussels" Jean Claude Van Damme, a much more made-to-order 80s action icon. While actually what they call "a moderate success" during its theatrical run, Battle Creek Brawl was seen as a disappointment by both Warner Brothers and Jackie Chan, himself, who were literally expecting an Enter the Dragon-sized hit. Same-same with Golden Harvest in Asia – the film did OK, but not nearly as well as they had hoped. However, the film (finally!) found its audience a few years later with mid-80s Cinemax viewers, for whom Battle Creek Brawl – by now re-titled simply The Big Brawl – was not only magnificent in its own weird right, but served as that "gateway drug" their high school D.A.R.E. Teachers had been warning them about, to the magnificence that is Jackie Chan!

About the Author
Jason McNeil is deeply ashamed to admit that, before sitting down to write this piece, he was unaware that H.B. "Hard Boiled" Haggerty (Battle Creek Brawl) and The Great John L (Breaker! Breaker!) were two entirely different people. He's going to go stand in the corner, now, and think about what he's done.

(While he's doing that, you should go watch him on Stars-Stunts-Action! now streaming on multiple platforms. Really – there's this whole thing in one episode where Bai Ling says she used to be a panther in a previous life and stays in shape by having "lots and lots of sex!" Then there are explosions. Its a fun watch.)

Jason McNeil

COLLECTING JACKIE CHAN japanese EPs

By Michael Nesbitt

During the 1970s, Japan saw a multitude of Bruce Lee released EPs hitting the shelves, and as the decade drew to a close, the Bruce Lee craze began to wane. However, movie-related records were still in high demand, and action movie fans were always on the lookout for new titles being released. The main reason for Bruce Lee's decline in the memorabilia market was because of the lack of new material available, so they tried to find a new Asian action star to focus on. During the late 1970s, a new martial arts actor was on the verge of becoming a superstar, a hopeful contender to the Bruce Lee throne.

Like most Chinese actors of the period, Jackie Chan began his career as a stuntman, even working in some Bruce Lee movies. And by the late 1970s, Chan had already starred in a number of low budget traditional style Kung Fu films, but it wasn't until the 1978 movie, Snake in the Eagle's Shadow, that Chan got his big break. The director of the movie, Yuen Woo-ping, allowed Chan the freedom to choreograph his own action scenes, and with its release, the Kung Fu Comedy genre was born, and Jackie Chan was the King. That same year, Drunken Master was also released in cinemas across Asia, and it was clear to all that Jackie Chan was destined to become a legend. Before long Jackie Chan memorabilia started appearing in stores all over the world, and, like Bruce Lee before him, record companies began releasing Jackie Chan records.

The first Jackie Chan EP to be released was the soundtrack for Drunken Master in 1979. This was soon followed up with other movie soundtracks, in fact, as soon as Jackie had made a movie during the 1980s, shortly after its release an EP would appear in music stores. One thing Jackie Chan could do that Bruce Lee couldn't, was that he could actually sing, and he would later become a singing sensation in the East. In the late 1980s, the music industry saw a major change within its industry, as records were becoming obsolete, as the Compact Disc (CD) took over. In 1988, the final Jackie Chan EP was put up for sale; this was the soundtrack for Dragons Forever, and every title thereafter was released on CD. In this second article on collecting Japanese EP records, we take a comprehensive look at all the Jackie Chan titles released in Japan.

Page 34   Eastern Heroes Jackie Chan Special Edition

THE JACKIE CHAN EP RECORD LIST
シャッキー チェン

Title: Drunken Fist, Drunken Monkey (Drunken Master)
Year: 1979
Label: See-Saw
Side A: Kung Fu Confusion
Side B: Tipsy Cute Guy
Info: The first Jackie Chan EP to be released in Japan. Taken from the soundtrack of Drunken Master.

Title: Crazy Monkey
Year: 1980
Label: Express
Side A: Crazy Monkey
Side B: Monkey Man
Info: Taken from the soundtrack of The Fearless Hyena.

Title: Battle Creek Brawl
Year: 1980
Label: Victor
Side A: Training Montage
Side B: Uncle Herbert
Info: Music is composed by Lalo Schifrin, who also did the Enter the Dragon soundtrack.

Title: Spiritual Kung Fu
Year: 1980
Label: Columbia
Side A: China Girl
Side B: Maria Madalena
Info: There were two different EP releases on the Columbia label for Spiritual Kung Fu, both having different B Sides.

Title: Spiritual Kung Fu
Year: 1980
Label: Columbia
Side A: China Girl
Side B: Everybody Fightin'
Info: This is the second Columbia release taken from the Jackie Chan movie Spiritual Kung Fu.

Title: : Cannonball Run
Year: 1981
Label: Victor
Side A: The Cannonball
Side B: Just for the Hell of It
Info: Taken from the soundtrack of the American made movie Cannonball Run.

Title: Miracle Fighter
Year: 1981
Label: Columbia
Side A: Miracle Fighter
Side B: Technotech Kung Fu
Info: Two fan inspired songs done by artists called Mojo and MFB. The cover image is taken from Battle Creek Brawl. It has Jackie's voice on the EP.

	**Title**: The Young Master - Flexi Disc **Year**: 1981 **Label**: Towa **Side A**: Message From Jackie **Side B**: Theme From The Young Master **Info**: This was a free giveaway promo flexi-disc for people who bought advanced movie tickets for the March 21, 1981 premiere of The Young Master.
	**Title**: Kung Fu Fighting Man **Year**: 1981 **Label**: Victor **Side A**: Kung Fu Fighting Man **Side B**: Fighting Kim (Instrumental) **Info:** This is the original soundtrack from the Young Master.
	**Title**: Shaolin Wooden Men **Year**: 1981 **Label**: Columbia **Side A**: Miracle Guy **Side B**: Broken Blossom **Info**: Taken from the soundtrack of Shaolin Wooden Men.
	**Title**: Dragon Lord **Year**: 1982 **Label**: Victor **Side A**: Dragon Lord **Side B**: The Joker Went Wild **Info**: Music performed by 'Time Five and Kung Fu Express'. Taken from the soundtrack of Dragon Lord.
	**Title**: Dragon Fist **Year**: 1982 **Label**: Columbia **Side A**: Dragon Fist **Side B**: Dragon Fist: Do Or Die **Info**: Taken from the original soundtrack of Dragon Fist.
	**Title**: Marianne **Year**: 1983 **Label**: Elektra **Side A**: Marianne **Side B**: Hello Happy Song **Info**: Both songs are sung by Jackie Chan in Japanese.
	**Title**: The Dragon Attack **Year**: 1983 **Label**: Philips **Side A:** Danger Love **Side B:** If You Turn Around, It's Jealousy **Info**: Music taken form the soundtrack of Fantasy Mission Force.

Title: Snake and Crane Arts of Shaolin
Year: 1983
Label: Columbia
Side A: Dangerous Eyes
Side B: The Moonless Night
Info: Taken from the soundtrack of Snake and Crane Arts of Shaolin.

Title: Cunning Monkey
Year: 1983
Label: Columbia
Side A: Cunning Monkey
Side B: Monkey's on the Loose
Info: Taken from the soundtrack of Half A Loaf of Kung Fu.

Title: Cannonball Run Part 2
Year: 1983
Label: Victor
Side A: Power On
Side B: Power On Part 2
Info: Taken from the soundtrack of the American made movie Cannonball Run 2. Music performed by The Kung Fu Express.

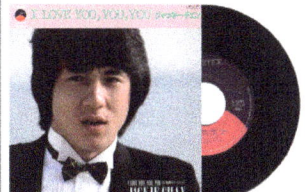

Title: I Love You, You, You
Year: 1984
Label: Elektra
Side A: I Love You, You, You
Side B: I Love You, You, You
Info: The A Side is sung in Japanese, and the B Side is sung in Chinese.

Title: Jackie: Heart and Gift
Year: 1984
Label: Elektra
Picture EP
Side A: I Love You, You, You
Side B: Heart is Yes
Green EP
Side A: I Love You, You, You
Side B: Heart is Yes
Info: This EP has two records, one is a picture disc, and the other is a Green disc. Both have the same tracks, with the Green EP being instrumental version. This EP comes with a gatefold sleeve, lyrics sheet, sticker sheet, pin-up and notepad.

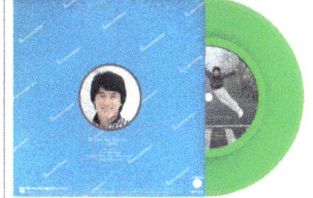

Title: To Kill With Intrigue
Year: 1984
Label: Columbia
Side A: To Kill With Intrigue
Side B: I Never Said It's Forever
Info: From the soundtrack of To Kill With Intrigue. The record is see-through, and has photos from the movie on the labels.

Title: Project A
Year: 1984
Label: Elektra
Side A: Project A
Side B: Project A (Instrumental)
Info: This is from the original soundtrack of the movie.

Title: Heart is Yes
Year: 1984
Label: Elektra
Side A: Heart is Yes
Side B: Movie Star
Info: The A Side is sung by Jackie in Japanese, and the B Side is sung in English. Includes a foldout poster of Jackie on a skateboard.

Title: Super Superstar (Winners and Sinners)
Year: 1984
Label: Canyon
Side A: Super Superstar
Side B: Angel
Info: The music is taken from the soundtrack of Winners and Sinners.

Title: Spartan X
Year: 1984
Label: Victor
Side A: Spartan X
Side B: Battle In Old Castle
Info: Music taken from the soundtrack of Wheels on Meals.

Title: The Police Story
Year: 1985
Label: Victor
Side A: Story of A Hero (Theme)
Side B: The Sexy Tape
Info: The B Side has a duet sung by Jackie Chan and Brigette Lin.

Title: Tokyo Saturday Night
Year: 1985
Label: Elektra
Side A: Tokyo Saturday Night
Side B: China Blue
Info: Taken from the soundtrack of the Jackie Chan movie Heart of the Dragon aka First Mission.

Title: My Lucky Stars
Year: 1985
Label: Canyon
Side A: Lucky Overture
Side B: Farewell Baikal
Info: Taken from the movie soundtrack of My Lucky Stars.

Title: The Protector
Year: 1985
Label: Victor
Side A: Prelude From The Protector
Side B: Quiet Night In Manhattan
Info: There were two EPs released for the Protector, one on the Victor label and the other on the Seven Seas label.

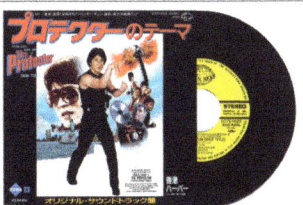	**Title**: The Protector **Year**: 1985 **Label**: Seven Seas **Side A**: The Protector (Main Title) **Side B**: Hong Kong Harbour **Info**: This EP includes a foldout poster of Jackie from The Protector.
	**Title**: : Thunder Arm (Armour of God) **Year**: 1986 **Label**: Canyon **Side A**: Lorelel **Side B**: Friend of Mine **Info**: Taken from the movie soundtrack of Armour of God. Songs performed by Alan Tam, who also starred in the movie alongside Jackie Chan.
	**Title**: Project A Part 2 **Year**: 1987 **Label**: Victor **Side A**: Project A Part 2 **Side B**: Project A Part 2 (Instrumental) **Info**: The song was written by Michael Lai, who also appeared in a number of Jackie Chan movies including, Project A Parts 1 and 2.
	**Title**: : No Problem (Seven Lucky Stars) **Year**: 1987 **Label**: Elektra **Side A**: No problem **Side B**: No problem (instrumental) **Info**: Sung in Cantonese. Taken form the soundtrack of Seven Lucky Stars aka Twinkle Twinkle Lucky Stars.
	**Title**: Luscious Night Song **Year**: 1988 **Label**: Elektra **Side A**: Luscious Night Song (Love Serenade Cantonese Version) **Side B**: Southern Cruise (Cantonese version) **Info**: Both tracks sung by Jackie Chan and Naoko Kawai.
	**Title**: Serenade of Love **Year**: 1988 **Label**: Columbia **Side A**: Serenade of Love **Side B**: Southern Cruise **Info**: Both songs sung by Jackie Chan and Naoko Kawai.
	**Title**: Cyclone Z (Dragons Forever) **Year**: 1988 **Label**: Victor **Side A**: Theme From Cyclone Z **Side B**: Theme From Cyclone Z (instrumental) **Info**: Music from the soundtrack of Cyclone Z aka Dragons Forever. The theme song on this EP is sung by Jackie Chan and Anita Mui.

COLLECTING JACKIE CHAN Japanese movie flyers

By Michael Nesbitt

Over the past four decades, there have been many countries that have sold Jackie Chan memorabilia, from Britain to America, from Hong Kong to Russia, there are literally thousands upon thousands of merchandise available. However, there is one country that stands out from most of these for the sheer quality and quantity of memorabilia they have released.

Japanese Jackie Chan memorabilia is truly breath-taking and some of it is unique only to Japan, one of these being the Japanese movie flyer. Like most other countries, Japan has released press books, promo photos, lobby cards, posters and various other pieces of merchandise to promote movies. However, the Japanese movie flyer is nearly solely unique to Japan itself. With fantastic imagery, and a distinctive writing style, their movie flyers, just like their posters, can be beautiful and fascinating at the same time, making them highly collectable within the action movie genre.

The Japanese movie flyers, which are typically B5 (7x10) in size, are usually sent to cinemas a month or two before the movie is released, the flyers would be laid out in the cinema lobby of a Japanese theatre prior to the showing of the movie that it is advertising. These were free to take for anyone who visited the cinema, and if there were any flyers left the day before the movie's release, the cinema would dispose of them. They were simply there to promote the movie before the release date.

Depending on how popular the movie was, there could be two or three different styles of flyers released. Usually the flyer itself would have a blank space at the bottom; this is where some of the larger cinema complexes could put their name, movie release date, location, and other bits of useful information. Some of them could also be stamped with the information. If a flyer has the white strip at the bottom blank, these were usually from the smaller more independent cinemas.

The most highly collectable flyers are the local variations that were produced by the theatre companies themselves, rather than the movie companies. These would normally be found in small towns and rural areas in Japan. These flyers are hard to find, and demand a high price.

Jackie Chan's popularity within Japan, meant that most of his movies were released in cinemas, and subsequently flyers were produced to promote them. Most of these flyers where portrait in style, however there is a selection of Jackie Chan flyers that were in landscape format, these would normally be flyers that were for a showing of a double feature, meaning two movies shown directly one after the other. Instead of putting these double feature movie flyers in the main section, I have put them at the end of the article, as I believe they deserve their own section simply for their uniqueness.

MOVIE FLYERS 1976 - 1981

1976 Shaolin Wooden Men

1977 To Kill with Intrigue

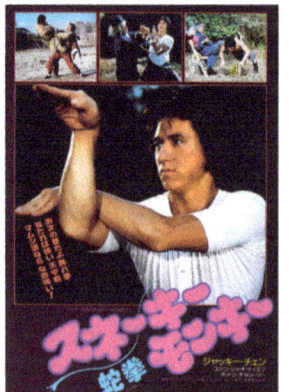
1978 Snake in the Eagles Shadow

1978 Snake & Crane Arts of Shaolin

1978 Half a Loaf of Kung Fu (A)

1978 Half a Loaf of Kung Fu (B)

1978 Drunken Master (A)

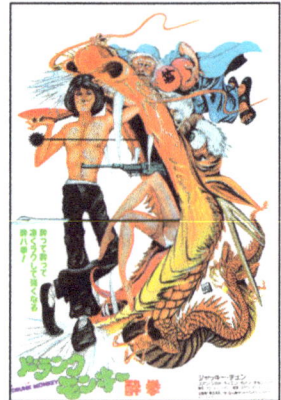
1978 Drunken Master (B)

1978 Spiritual Kung Fu

1979 The Fearless Hyena

1979 Dragon Fist

1980 The Young Master

1980 Battle Creek Brawl (A)

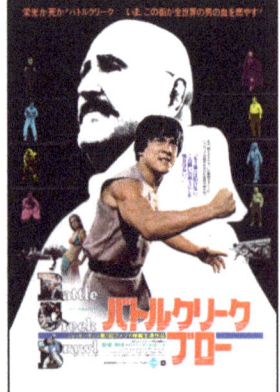
1980 Battle Creek Brawl (B)

1980 Battle Creek Brawl (C)

1981 The Cannon Ball Run (A)

MOVIE FLYERS 1981 - 1985

1981 The Cannon Ball Run (B)

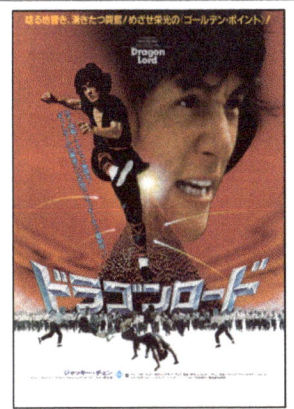
1982 Dragon Lord (A)

1982 Dragon Lord (B)

1983 Fantasy Mission Force

1983 The Fearless Hyena part 2

1983 Winner and Sinners (A)

1983 Winner and Sinners (B)

1983 Project A (A)

1983 Project A (B)

1984 The Cannonball Run 2 (A)

1984 The Cannonball Run 2 (B)

1984 The Cannonball Run 2 (C)

1984 Wheels on Meals (A)

1984 Wheels on Meals (B)

1985 My Lucky Stars (A)

1985 My Lucky Stars (B)

MOVIE FLYERS 1985 - 1991

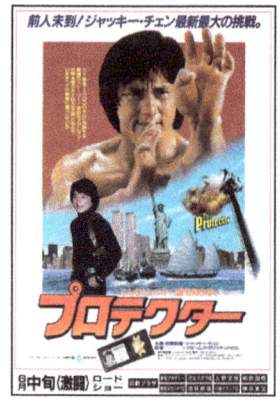
1985 The Protector (A)

1985 The Protector (B)

1985 Twinkle Twinkle Lucky Stars

1985 First Misson

1985 Police Story (A)

1985 Police Story (B)

1986 Armour of God (A)

1986 Armour of God (B)

1987 Project A Part 2 (A)

1987 Project A Part 2 (B)

1988 Dragons Forever

1988 Police Story Part 2 (A)

1988 Police Story Part 2 (B)

1989 Miracles

1990 Island of Fire

1991 Operation Condor (A)

MOVIE FLYERS 1991 - 1998

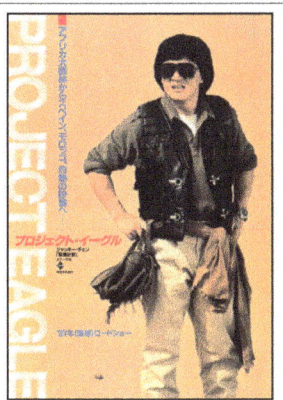
1991 Operation Condor (B)

1992 Twin Dragons (A)

1992 Twin Dragons (B)

1992 Police Story 3 (A)

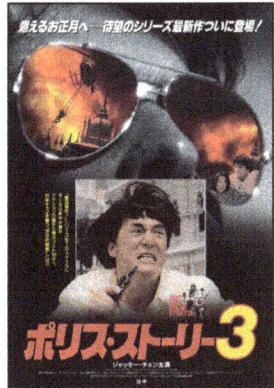
1992 Police Story 3 (B)

1993 City Hunter

1993 Crime Story

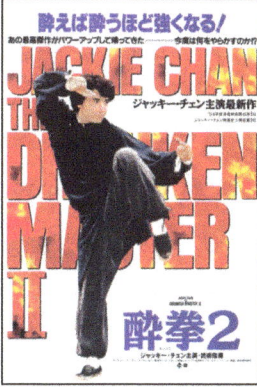
1994 Drunken Master 2 (A)

1994 Drunken Master 2 (B)

1995 Rumble in the Bronx

1995 Thunderbolt (A)

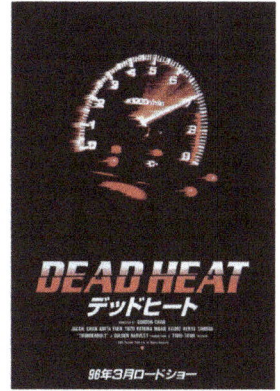
1995 Thunderbolt (B)

First Strike (A)

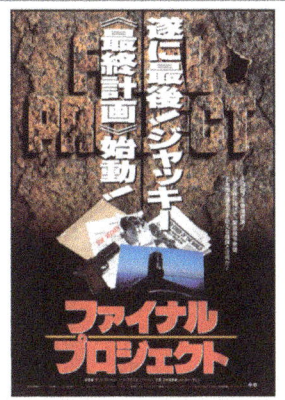
First Strike (B)

1997 Mr Nice Guy

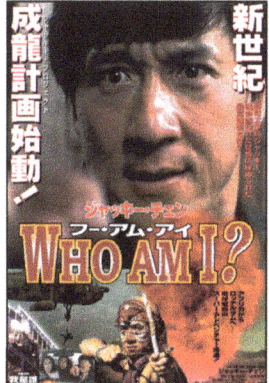
1998 Who Am I

MOVIE FLYERS 1998 - 2004

1998 Rush Hour (A)

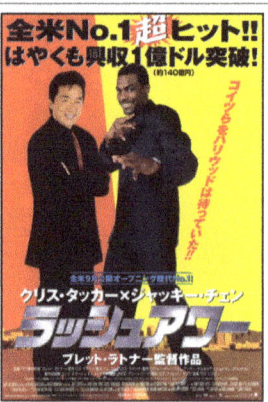
1998 Rush Hour (B)

1999 Gorgeous

1999 Gen Y Cops

2000 Shanghai Noon

2001 The Accidental Spy

2001 Rush Hour 2 (A)

2001 Rush Hour 2 (B)

2002 The Tuxedo

2003 Shanghai Knights

2003 The Twins Effect (A)

2003 The Twins Effect (B)

2003 Traces of a Dragon

2003 The Medallion

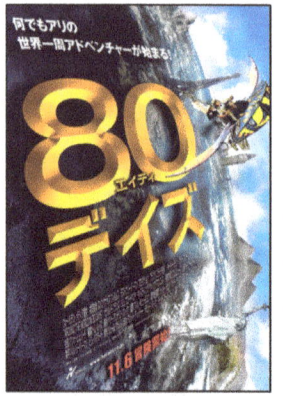
2004 Around the World in 80 Days

2004 The Twins Effect 2

MOVIE FLYERS 2004 - 20211

2004 New Police Story (A)

2004 New Police Story (B)

2005 The Myth (A)

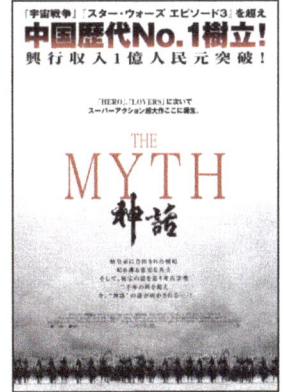
2005 The Myth (B)

2006 Robin-B-Hood

2007 Rush Hour 3 (A)

2007 Rush Hour 3 (B)

2008 The Forbidden Kingdom

2008 Kung Fu Panda (A)

2008 Kung Fu Panda (B)

2009 Shinjuku Incident

2010 The Spy Next Door

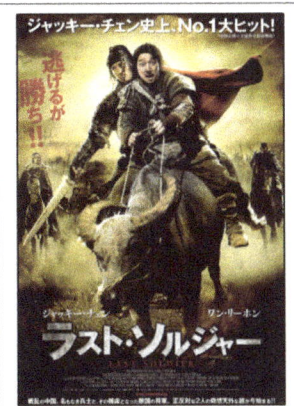
2010 Little Big Soldier

2010 The Karate Kid

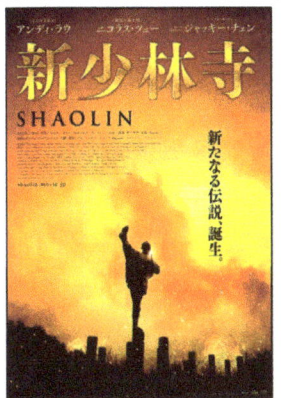
2011 Shaolin (A)

2011 Shaolin (B)

MOVIE FLYERS 2011 - 2017

2011 Kung Fu Panda 2 (A)

2011 Kung Fu Panda 2 (B)

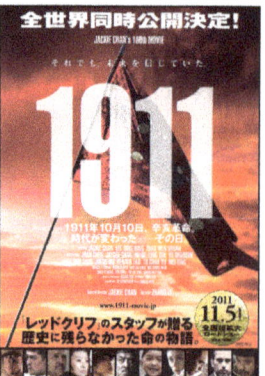
2011 - 1911 (A)

2011 - 1911 (B)

2012 Chinese Zodiac (A)

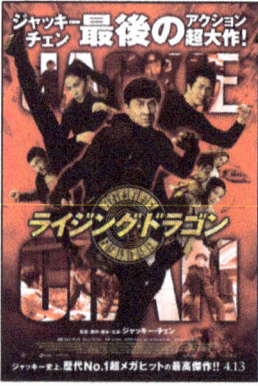
2012 Chinese Zodiac (B)

2013 Police Story: Lockdown

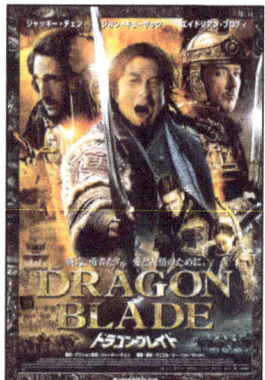
2015 Dragon Blade (A)

2015 Dragon Blade (B)

2016 Kung Fu Panda 3

2016 Skiptrace (A)

2016 Skiptrace (B)

2016 Railroad Tigers

2017 Kung Fu Yoga (A)

2017 Kung Fu Yoga (B)

2017 Ninjago (A)

MOVIE FLYERS 2017 - 2020

2017 Ninjago (B)

2017 The Foreigner

2017 Bleeding Steel

2017 Namiya

2019 The Knight of Shadows

2019 Iron Mask

2019 The Climbers

2020 Vanguard

DOUBLE FEATURE MOVIE FLYERS

A popular aWracCon in most cinemas, were double features, these were two movies played back to back, one straight aRer the other. The following flyers are some of the Jackie Chan Double Features that were shown from 1976 to 1992. Both movies were usually released within a year of each other and would normally consist of the most popular movies of the time. The movie flyer on the first page is from 1979, which features Jackie Chan's Drunken Master, and Bunta Sugawara's Trucker Yaro IX A 5000 Km Run, this is the only flyer that is in a portrait style, all of the other double feature movie flyers are in a landscape format.

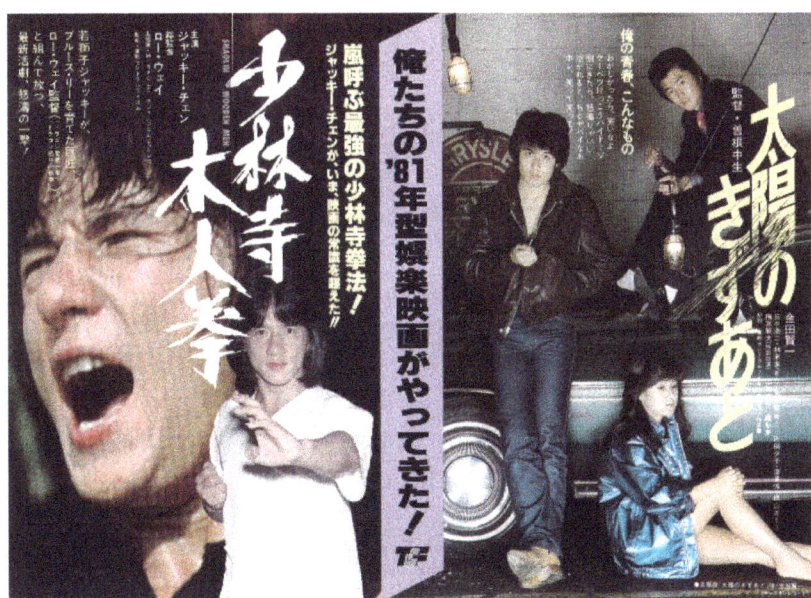

1976 Shaolin Wooden Men
1976 Scars of the Sun

Page 49   Eastern Heroes Jackie Chan Special Edition

DOUBLE FEATURE MOVIE FLYERS 1979 - 1992

1979 Target
1979 Fearless Hyena

1981 Endless love
1981 Cannonball Run

1982 The Cunnins IQ=0
1982 Dragon Lord

1983 Fearless Hyena 2
1983 Fist of the North Star

1984 Tha Cannonball Run 2
1984 Misunderstood

1984 Heavenly Bodies
1984 Wheels on Meals

1985 A Penguins memory: Tale of Happiness
1985 The Protector

1985 Cocoon
1985 Police Story

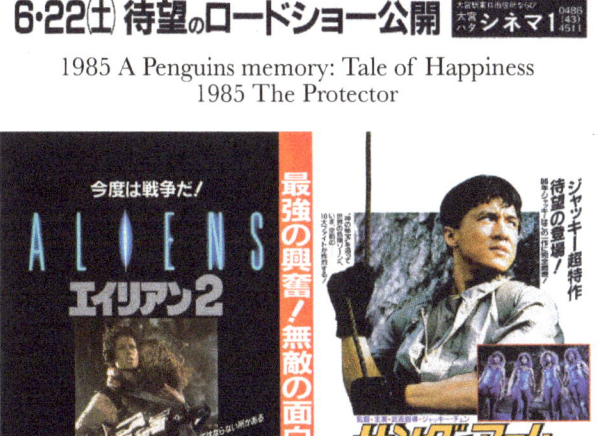

1986 Aliens
1986 Armour of God

1987 The Drifting Classroom
1987 Project A Part 2

1988 Dragons Forever
1988 Top Dog

1988 Police Story 2
1988 White Lion

1990 Teenage Mutant Ninja Turtles
1991 Operation Condor (AOG 2)

1992 Freejack
1992 Twin Dragons

1992 Universal Solider
1992 Police Story 3

BUD SPENCER & JACKIE CHAN
WHAT COULD HAVE BEEN...

By Thorsten Boose

Hands up, who still remembers the days before the internet and streaming services? Back then films were either made for cinema, television with annoying commercial breaks or for worn VHS tapes in video stores. The video store charm of yesteryear will never rise again, and that is precisely why many people fondly remember this time. Even if the blockbusters from Hollywood generated sales in the video stores, of course, the niche genres or former grindhouse cinema strips were never to be underestimated, especially in (West) Germany. Be it action films of the C category, 80s splatters or fast paced kung fu flicks with Jacky Chan from the Far East - the 80s and 90s offered a potpourri of cinematic entertainment.
One type of film was particularly popular in Germany, the films with Bud Spencer and Terence Hill. Videos of Italian action comedies with Bud Spencer such as "Double Trouble" (1984), "Go For It" (1983) or "Watch Out, We're Mad" (1974) sold like hot cakes. Not least because of the type of dubbing that is called Schnodderdeutsch in Germany.

Schnodderdeutsch as a subgenre
Schnodderdeutsch is a mixture of rough and funny pub language paired with 60s and 70s youth jargon and goes back to the German dubbing pope Rainer Brandt, dialogue author and dubbing actor. The linguistic style is characterized by neologisms, apparent proverbs, style breaks, metaphors and other rhetorical stylistic elements that are creatively used by dialogue authors and voice actors. An example of a typical Schnodderdeutsch dubbing of a Jackie Chan movie, albeit a bit stripped down, would be "Police Story" (1985): „May, was ist, hast du dir den Stiez geprellt?" And many more quotes that are untranslatable. Other voice actors and dialogue writers who shaped Schnodderdeutsch are Karlheinz Brunnemann, Arne Elsholtz, Michael Richter and Heinz Petruo. That same Arne Elsholtz dubbed Jackie Chan in "Police Story" (1985). With this Schnodderdeutsch dubbing, this otherwise serious film stands out from its successors and gives Jackie's personal masterpiece an additional note of humour. Since these action comedies with Bud Spencer and Terence Hill were so successful in the cinemas and video stores (to this day even on German television), more and more producers and distributors wanted to work more closely with the two Italian film stars. The films were soon created especially for the "Schnodder German" market. In this way, a whole generation of German-speaking film fans was shaped and celebrates Schnodderdeutsch to this day.

And while Bud Spencer was traveling around the world in his films, at some point behind closed office doors the question arose whether he could not be muddled in a movie with a certain

Shadowman aka Powerman aka Superfighter named Jacky (!) Chan. According to Bud's scriptwriter at the

time, Lorenzo De Luca, it was possible.

Who is Bud Spencer?

Bud Spencer is born Carlo Pedersoli in Naples on October 31, 1929. His mother is Rina "Rosa" Facchetti, who comes from Brescia, and his father is the furniture manufacturer Alessandro Pedersoli. Just one year after starting school in 1936, Carlo makes his first swimming attempts and joins a swimming club. In 1943, the Second World War enters Naples. The Pedersolis furniture factory is destroyed in air raids by the Allies." *1

Carlo Pedersoli aka Bud Spencer celebrated many successes as a swimmer before his film career and competed in the Olympic Games for Italy several times. After his sports career, he married, had children and composed songs for a record company. He went into business for himself with a production company that mainly produced documentaries.

He did not see himself as an actor. Until director Giuseppe Colizzi gave him the lead role in the spaghetti western "God forgives… I don't!" (1967). The serious businessman didn't want to ruin his reputation by starring in a silly comedy, so he grew a beard without further ado.

„As a new name, Carlo chooses a combination of his then favourite actor Spencer Tracy and his favourite beer brand Budweiser: Bud Spencer is born." *1

The second major role in the film went to Mario Girotti, who also took a pseudonym: Terence Hill. Neither of them were convinced of a career in film, especially as the hype surrounding the once so successful spaghetti western was subsiding. But history should prove them wrong.

A certain Lorenzo De Luca grew up with the films by Bud Spencer and Terence Hill, who would later work with his idol several times and initiate an important meeting with Jackie Chan.

1 source: www.spencerhilldb.de (as of 12/2021)

Who is Lorenzo De Luca?
Lorenzo De Luca was born in Rome in 1963. His parents were both in the film business, so he ended up in this industry as

Lorenzo De Luca with Jackie Chan

well. Early on he wrote articles on films and published his first book on spaghetti westerns in 1987, followed by a series of books on Bruce Lee and kung fu films in general.
With Bud Spencer, his idol, he first worked together in 1991 as a screenwriter for the film "Detective Extralarge – Miami Killer" as part of a TV film series. His dream came true and other film and later book

projects with Bud Spencer followed. Bud Spencer's first autobiography, in collaboration with his friend and screenwriter Lorenzo De Luca, was published in Italy in 2010 under the title "Altrimenti mi arrabbio – La mia vita". Other joint books followed, which, like Bud Spencer's films, found numerous grateful buyers, especially in Germany. When a certain Jackie Chan was to receive his honorary Oscar in 2016, Lorenzo De Luca decided to give a little more insight into an anecdote from Bud Spencer's autobiography, namely how he and Jackie's manager Willie Chan spoke about a joint film project with Bud Spencer.

Bud what about Jackie?
Would that have been possible, a joint film with Jackie Chan and Bud Spencer? According to Lorenzo De Luca, such a project was even discussed for years. How this came about is explained in detail by the scriptwriter in an internet article dated September 16, 2016:
„Since about the late 1980s, when I managed to contact him through the Hong Kong Film Festival, Jackie had sent me press books, autographed photos, and other material, and I in turn had him a copy of my fourth book ("Bruce Lee. Il

ritorno del drago", ed. Mediterranee), in which an entire chapter revolved around him, clever! He understood Italian as well as I understood Cantonese, zero, but he had good eyesight and the photos in the book said it all."

*2 Lorenzo De Luca goes on to say that he got the chance to meet Jackie Chan in person years later. At this meeting Jackie asked him what was going on with Bud Spencer, which clearly surprised Lorenzo.

„I was happy and surprised: happy because I worked for Bud the most, and surprised because I didn't know Jackie was his admirer. I thought a movie with them would be a hit." *2

That must have been 1995, as a joint photo shows. At this point in time, "Rumble In The Bronx" (1995) had box office successes and slowly but surely ensured that Hollywood got back to Jackie Chan. There wasn't much time for a joint project between Bud Spencer and Jackie Chan – if it wasn't too late.

Screenwriter Lorenzo De Luca knew this and immediately sat down with Bud's son Giuseppe Pedersoli to discuss a joint film project. First, the character differences between the two actors had to be worked out in order to find a plot that both could authentically bring to the big screen. Two originals need a common goal, which connects them in the story.

„More [time] passed between the actual writing, the adaptation in English, the shipping, and finally the very slow response from Golden Harvest, the company Jackie was representing." *2

But Golden Harvest and the JC Group weren't slow, on the contrary. Meanwhile, "Rush Hour" (1998) was released and catapulted Jackie into megastar orbit, where he appeared out of reach for Lorenzo and Bud Spencer. Nevertheless, the Italian filmmaker persisted and wrote his manuscript. The title of this screenplay, which was initially written in Italian, was "L'Impero de Draghi" (English: "Empire of Dragons") and was supposed to be about the ancient Romans in China. It was based on the 2005 novel of the same name by the Italian writer Valerio Massimo Manfredi. When Lorenzo De Luca travelled to Hong Kong in 2007 while working on the documentary "Dragonland - L'urlo di Chen terrorizza ancora l'occidente" (2008), he paid a visit to the JC Group and Willie Chan, Jackie Chan's manager. „Good Willie Chan asked me to sit down immediately. Although many years had passed, he had not forgotten me. He told me Jackie was in Paris for 'Rush Hour 3' and I gave him a copy of the script in English, suggesting a productive partnership with Aurelio De Laurentiis. Willie smiled warmly, but it was clear that in order to propose something to Jackie you had to go through agents and lawyers by now. Nothing came of that." *2 In the meantime, it was clear to Lorenzo De Luca that he had to put his dream of a film with his idol and now good friend Bud Spencer and Jackie Chan aside. It is not known whether Willie Chan kept the script for "Empire Of Dragons". But a few years later, "Dragon Blade" (2015) was released in which the ancient Romans invaded China. A huge Chinese production starring Hollywood stars John Cusack and Adrien Brody alongside Jackie Chan.

"Could that be a coincidence?", Lorenzo De Luca also asked the question in the aforementioned internet article from 2016, when "Dragon Blade" just ended with less convincing box office numbers, according to him. At least as far as the Hong Kong sales are concerned, this is correct. Because with a budget of around 65 million US dollars, ("Dragon Blade") grossed over 117 million US dollars in the People's Republic of China alone. And since Jackie Chan co-produced the film with his company Sparkle Roll Media, it

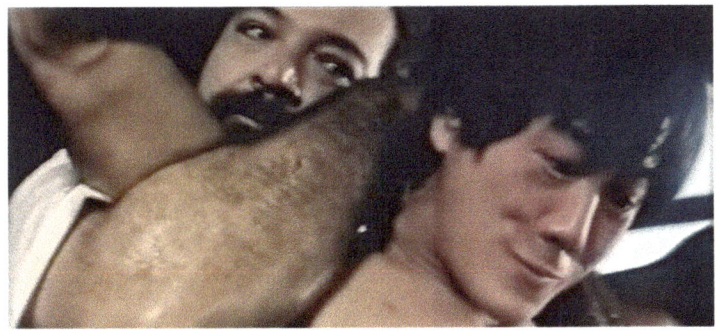

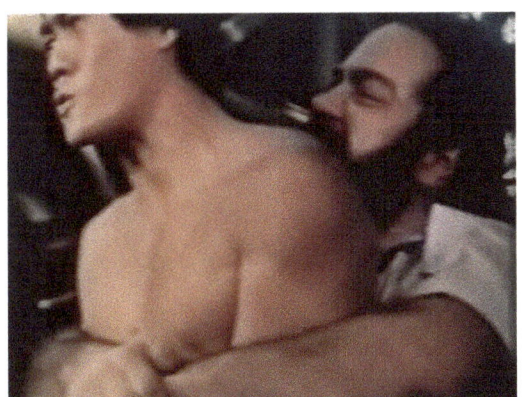

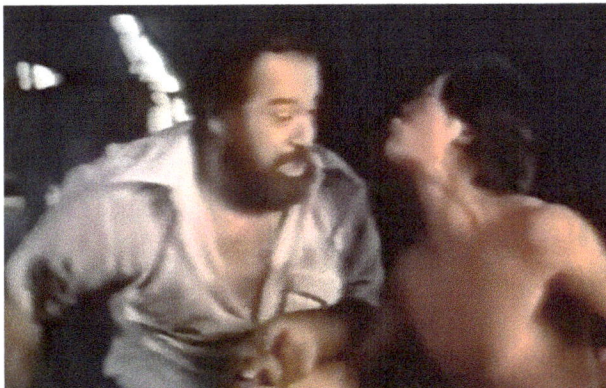
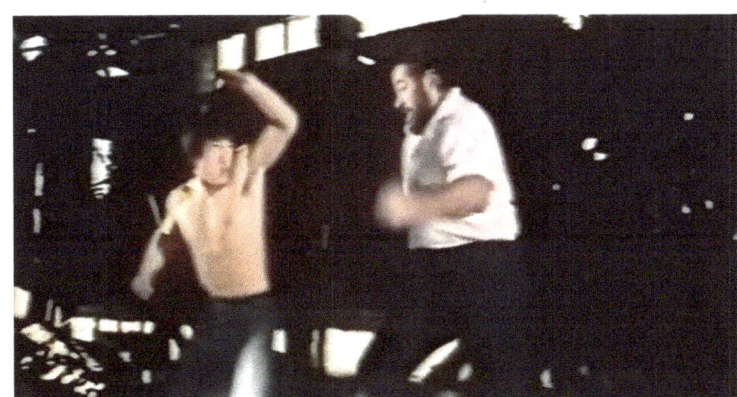
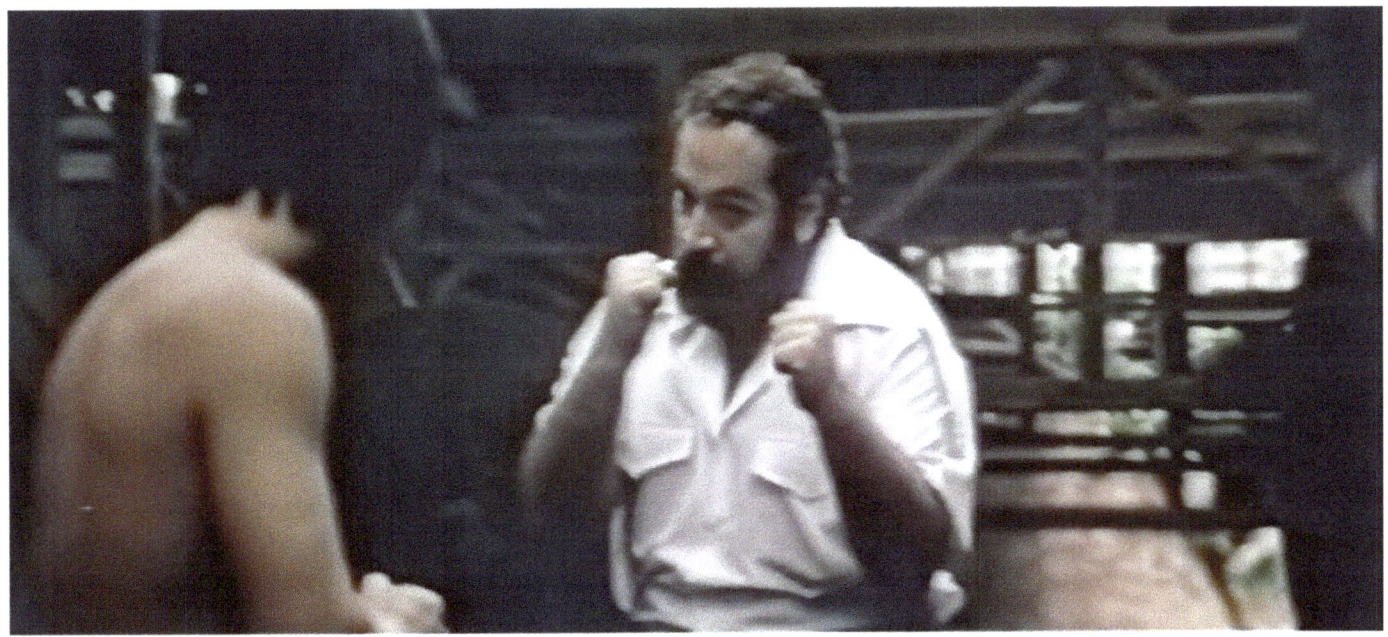

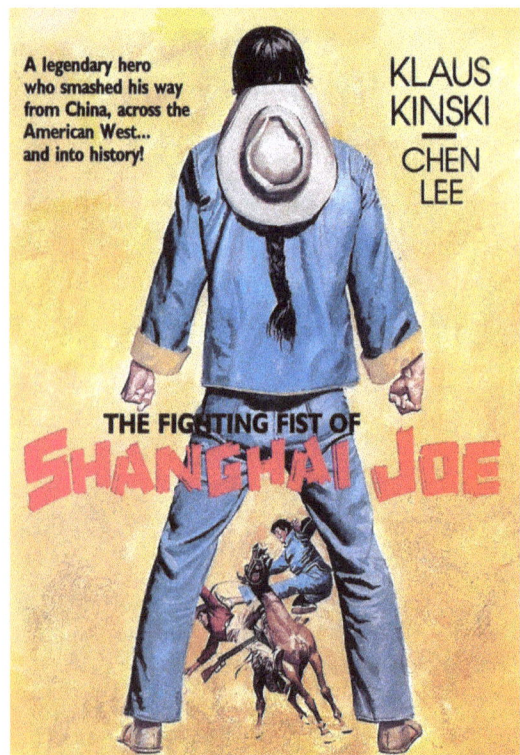

can be seen as a well-calculated investment. Where I personally never considered collaboration between Jackie Chan and Bud Spencer possible, regardless of whether it was in the late 1970s, mid 1980s or early 1990s, I at least understand the arguments of some film buffs that could actually speak in favour of it. Lorenzo De Luca explains it like what Bud Spencer did in the west, Jackie Chan did in the east, namely funny action comedy in a very

unique, unprecedented style that was difficult to copy. Imitation, as Lorenzo De Luca writes in Bud Spencer's autobiography "In achtzig Jahren um die Welt – Der zweite Teil meiner Autobiografie", is in my opinion out of the question, either from the one or the other point of view.

„[…] Also in Hong Kong, the kung fu star Jackie Chan teamed up with a film partner in the 1980s, when he was still a blank sheet in the West. He wanted to break away from the cliché of his previous films and give his career a new direction. Together with Sammo Hung, he founded a duo that was similar to our constellation: the fat and the thin who

fight fights full of acrobatic interludes, but in which nobody ever dies. Then Yuen Biao joined and the duo became a trio.

When Jackie Chan came to Rome many years later, he met my co-author Lorenzo De Luca, who had been in correspondence with him and his manager Willie Chan for years. Not least because Lorenzo used to write articles and books about his films when he was still relatively unknown. Without knowing that he was working with me, Jackie Chan asked Lorenzo during this visit: "What happened to Bud Spencer and Terence Hill?"

Our films, which he had seen on video cassette, had been the source of inspiration for his so-called "kung fu comedy" together with Buster Keaton and Chaplin." *3

I mean did he really? Jackie rarely or never mentioned Bud Spencer and Terence Hill in his career, never mind that the two are said to have had a lasting influence on his own cinematic work. Jackie Chan's style in particular resembles Chop Suey: "I lump everything together and see what comes out of it." This applies to both his fighting style and his film style. In his exorbitant filmography, he made use of classic silent film stars such as Buster Keaton and Harold Lloyd as well as modern directors such as Steven Spielberg. The best learn from the best. So it is possible that Jackie watched Bud Spencer films – and vice versa! Certain trends can take place in different parts of the world at the same time, as the history of various technological and scientific inventions teaches us. Keyword Zeitgeist. But in the book Lorenzo De Luca talks about another film project by his two childhood idols:

"Years ago, Lorenzo and Giuseppe had the glorious idea of pairing Bud and Jackie into a film duo. And with our different statures and natures, we could actually have made a wonderful duo. The two developed an incredibly funny story called "The Monk". It is about

a Chinese monk, a kung fu expert who, however, is quite inexperienced in all other areas of life and has never set foot outside of his Chinese monastery. He is suddenly catapulted to Rome, where he is supposed to take part in an important religious event. Once there, he rushes from one mess to the next and on the occasion also runs into me, a grouchy policeman about to retire. The two team up to beat up the usual villains while getting to know each other and gradually overcoming cultural differences. When I tell the plot, it sounds so simple. But writing a script is a time-consuming and stressful business. And when it finally stood and only had to be translated, Jackie Chan had just landed a huge hit in America with "Rush Hour" and became an unattainable Hollywood star. We sent the script to Hong Kong but never got a response. Nonetheless, the fact that we both, Terence, you and I, are known to actors who live almost on the other side of the world is a wonderful gift." *3

*2 source: "A novembre Jackie Chan riceverà l'Oscar alla carriera. Lorenzo De Luca ce lo racconta in esclusiva!"; released: 16th September, 2016 (www.mondospettacolo.com)
*3 source: " In achtzig Jahren um die Welt – Der zweite Teil meiner Autobiografie"; released: 15th March, 2012 (Schwarzkopf & Schwarzkopf).

Budsploitation and the Spaghetti Eastern
Let's travel back in time for a moment. It is 1973, a very young Jackie Chan tries his luck as a stuntman in Hong Kong and takes his first steps as a martial arts director. This year he takes on many jobs, at the moment he is working on a Hong Kong co-production with Italy called "Supermen Against the Orient" (1973).
The 19-year-old teaches his Hong Kong colleagues to be lenient with the Italian actors who are inexperienced in martial arts. It's just a job and it makes money. The action comedy's director, actually a Spaghetti Eastern, is a certain Bitto Albertini.
The film is not a real success, but today it is of course a coveted collector's item, especially among Jackie Chan fans, and was supposed to trigger a number of Spaghetti

Easterns back then – the fastest fists from the Far East should fight the strongest paws from the West. In the same year, the film "The Fighting Fists of Shanghai Joe" with Chen Lee, a Japanese actor (!) who embodies a Chinese in the Wild West, and Klaus Klinski, the eccentric German scandal actor of the 60s and 70s, are made.

"The Fighting Fists of Shanghai Joe" aka "My Name is Shanghai Joe" flops and yet in 1975 a kind of pseudo continuation appears under the title "Return of Shanghai Joe". In this German-Italian co-production, Klaus Kinski is playing once again the villain, but this time Shanghai Joe is played by Cheen Lie. His only film appearance ever. Another "star" is the actor Tommy Polgár, who already appeared in "My Name is Nobody" with Terence Hill and Henry Fonda. Visually very much based on Bud Spencer and actually spoken by Bud Spencer's voice Wolfgang Hess in the German dubbed version. "Return of Shanghai Joe" comes closest to a what could have been a joint film between Bud Spencer and Jackie Chan, at least in the 1970's style. Politically correctness did not exist at the time. By the way, it was directed by Bitto Albertini. If a formula works, people like to copy it, be it Brucesploitation, Jackiesploitation or Budsploitation. In the 1970s, several Bud Spencer copies were made with Paul L. Smith (known for his appearance as The Beast Rabban in "Dune" or Bluto in "Popeye"), including the 1977 Taiwanese flick "Return of the Tiger" with Bruce Li and Angela Mao. Another Spaghetti Eastern and probably one of the last ever made. A strange IMDb credit can be found on Paul L. Smith that builds a bridge to Jackie Chan: In "The Protector" from 1985 he is said to have played Mr. Booar. Whether a film starring Bud Spencer and Jackie Chan would have worked remains a mystery. Parallels in the cinematic style of the two are undeniable, albeit mostly minimal. The two originals channelled the Zeitgeist, which ultimately connected the different cultures. But that's a thing with parallels, they run alongside and never meet in a common goal.

Big thank you, to Lorenzo De Luca and Christian Sadjak for supporting me with pictures.

JACKIE CHAN'S Lucky Stars

THE TRAIDS VS THE HONG KONG FILM INDUSTRY...

By Simon Pritchard

During the 1980's and 1990's the Hong Kong film industry was at its peak. In the early 1990's the box office would take over $1 Billion (USD). The industry attracted a lot of attention including Hong Kong's organised crime syndicate, the Triads.

With hundreds of films made per year; films were easy to get financed back then without getting asked many questions. The Hong Kong film industry at the time was a 'guaranteed winner', so the Triads would use their elitist gains to fund films, as an efficient money laundering process which gave them quick and easy returns. As the industry grew, so did the Triad's wealth and greed.

The Triads saw the wealth of the cast and crew members and moved into exploitation. Philip Chan ("Twinkle, Twinkle, Lucky Stars", "Bloodsport", "Hard Boiled") once said: *"In the day-to-day filming, we were being extorted in the streets; they would demand anything from $50 (USD) to $2,000 (USD). Sometimes you would get two or three groups coming at different times. They would try to tamper with the equipment, they would obstruct filming, sometimes they would intimidate the actors. And it was very difficult to get police protection."*

To keep their reign over the film industry as long as possible, the Triads tried to control the industry. Andy Lau ("Infernal Affairs", "House of the Flying Daggers", "God of Gamblers") has said that his manager was held at gunpoint and was forced to sign Andy into a three-year film contract.

When intimidation did not work, The Triads would resort to violence even within their own organisation. In the early 1990's a popular Hong Kong singer, Anita Mui, got struck in the face publicly by film director and suspected Chinese 'Mainland' Triad member, Wong Long Lai, after she refused to sing for him. The day after, Wong Long Lai was attacked with a butcher's knife which he survived. Whilst in the hospital recovering, he was shot dead in the bed where he lay.

A year later the Hong Kong 'Traditional' Triad boss and professional race car driver, Andely "The Tiger of Wan Chai" Chan, was arrested for Wong Long Lai's murder. He was released without charge and was then shot dead at the Macau Grand Prix in 1993 along with one of his mechanics, Tse Chun-Fung.

It's been said that the vast majority of films were controlled directly or even in-directly by the Triads. As this type of behaviour was prevalent in the industry at the time, and no actor or director was immune even Jackie Chan.

Jackie has allegedly previously spoken about extortion and threats with other actors whilst having guns pointed at them. Jackie said in the South China Morning Post:

"In the past, when they bullied me, I hid in the United States. They opened fire at me once I got off the aeroplane. From that moment on, I needed to carry a gun every day when I went out. When I returned to Hong Kong and ate outside, more than twenty people surrounded me with melon knives."

"I pulled out a gun and had two more concealed. I told them they had been going too far and that I had been hiding from them. Later on, I confronted them with two guns and six grenades."

Jackie has never commented on the outcome of the confrontation. It is not also clear when this happened, but Jackie

originally made his first American film, "The Big Brawl", in 1980. Jackie then made "Cannonball Run" and its sequel in 1981 and 1984 respectively, then the Hong Kong / American made film "The Protector" in 1985. It was ten years until Jackie returned to America to make "Rumble in Bronx" before the success with "Rush Hour" in 1998. Between 1980 and 1995 Jackie starred, presented, produced, or directed 17 films in Hong Kong.

In the mid to late 1990's the Police protection started on filmsets, and the Police were infiltrating the gangs, in conjunction with the Hong Kong film industry starting to lose momentum, the Triads interests started to diminish. Hollywood was becoming more popular again, increases the prices of film production and reducing the profits in Hong Kong. Philip Chan believes there may still be a few Triads left in the industry but "If you are pretty successful then there is nothing that you cannot really master through proper business transactions. Why resort to something else?".

From world records, the moves, throwing himself of buildings, dodging bullets from gangsters, Jackie has a place in Cinema that will not be replicated.

APPRECIATE THE LOBBY

From the Jackie Chan Appreciation Facebook Group, we have a selection of fan made lobby cards. First up is a 35 card set specially made for the 35th anniversary of Police Story.

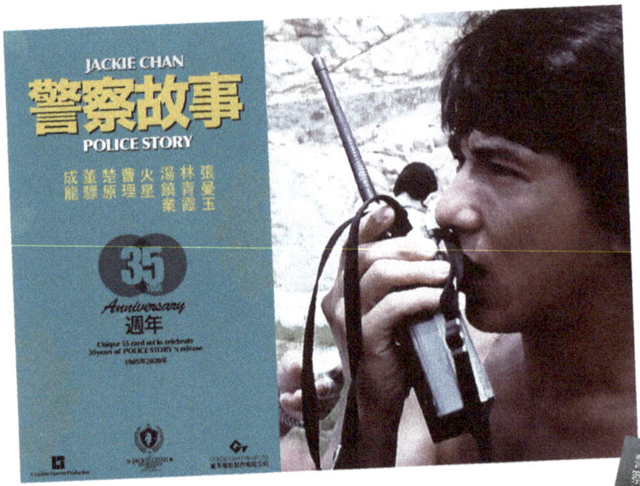

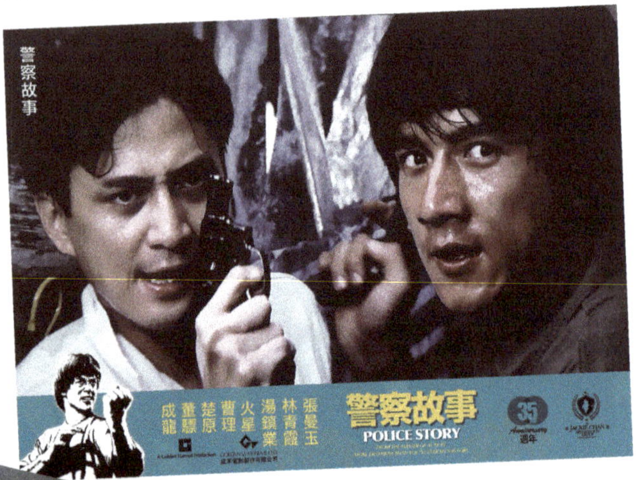

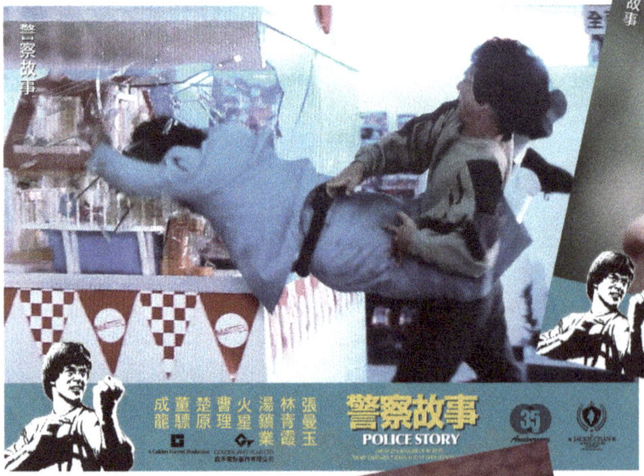

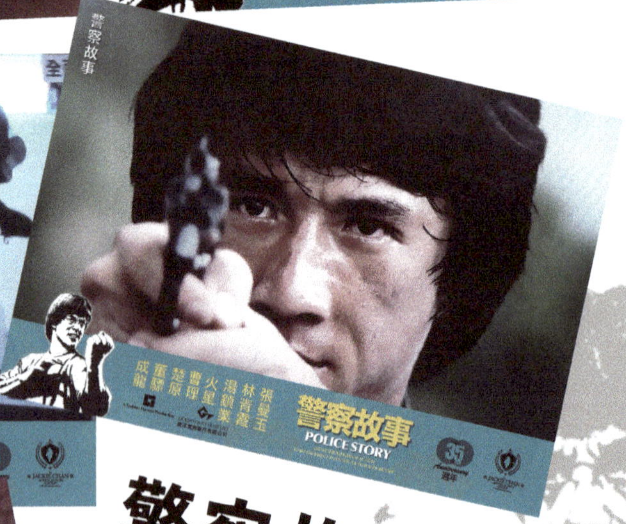

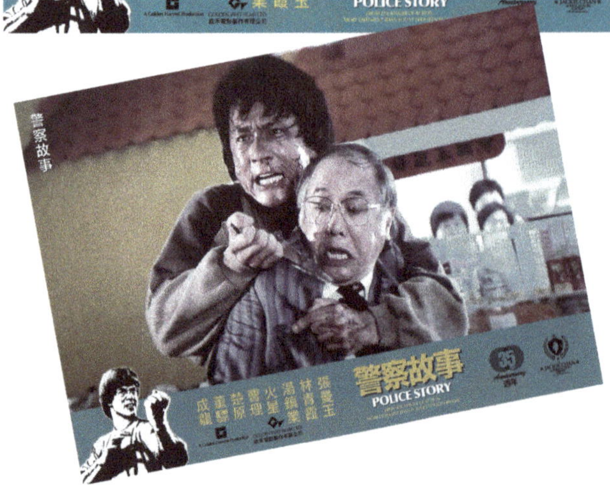

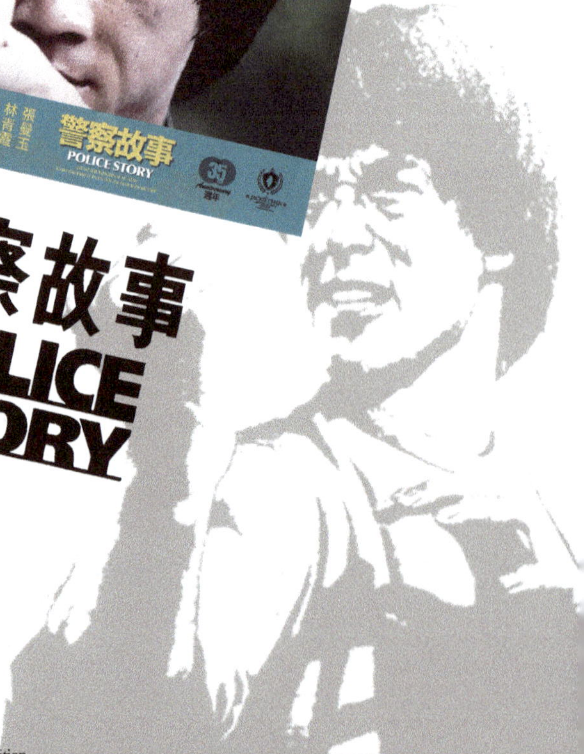

龍拳 DRAGON FIST

龍的心
FIRST MISSION

This was the first set we produced for the group. Paul selected some not so common images that we usually might see to go into this set, making it a bit more of a rarity.

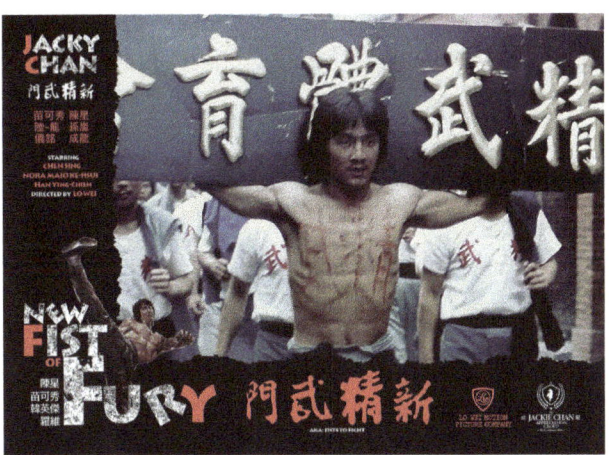

新精武門
NEW FIST OF FURY

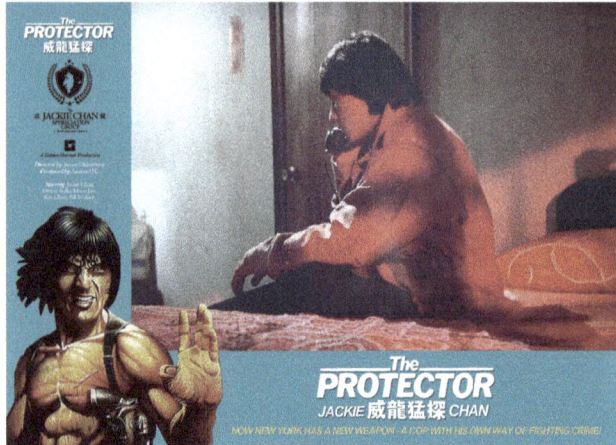

TO KILL WITH INTRIGUE

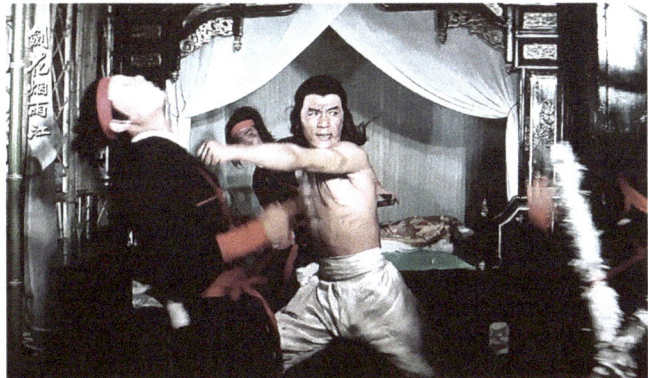

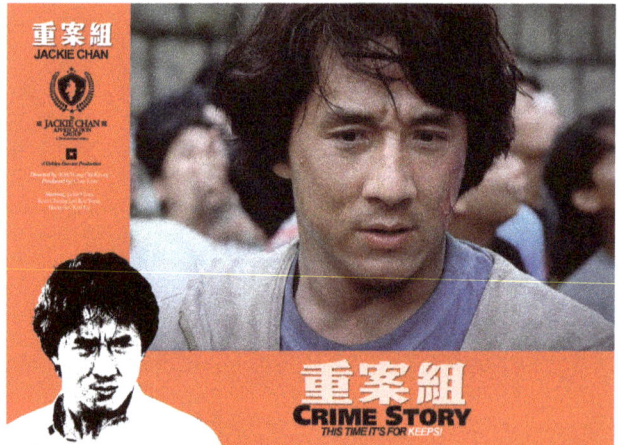

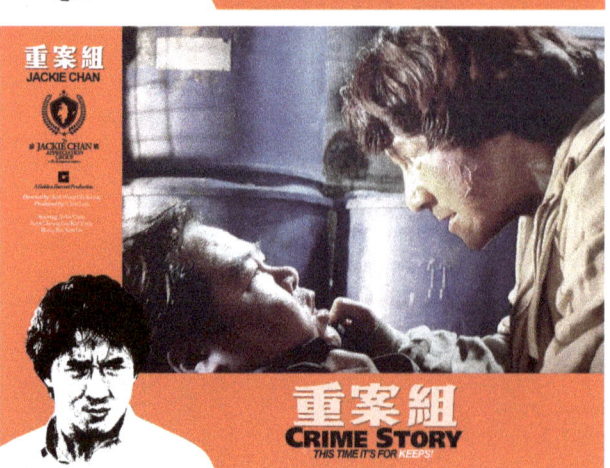

POSTER STORY

Alan Donkin — Professional Nobody

THE AUTHORS

Matt Routledge — Award-Winner

AD: Welcome to a poster article with a twist. Not Oliver, the cheeky Dickensian roustabout. Nor Tony, the Canadian ice hockey player nobody reading this will have ever heard of. Those are good twists, but not the twist I had in mind. The twist in mind saves me a lot of hassle. The last thing I could be arsed to do for this Jackie Chan special was another dry, frankly exhausting, whistle-stop tour of hundreds of cinematic posters for his worldwide movie releases. And there are, literally, hundreds. Sod that. Therefore, I considered a different angle. The genesis was thus: I was chatting over Messenger with my good friend Matt Routledge, whom I have known for several years (but never actually met – an oversight that needs correcting!). He's an all-round excellent chap; one of the good eggs in the scene. Moreover, he knows his onions. So, I decided to ask him if he'd agree to co-authoring a piece that is fundamentally a matey chat about Jackie's film posters. Graciously (and mercifully), he agreed.

The premise is this: I scour the internet, my own, and other peoples' collections, and compile a list of my favourite ten posters, along with a brief explanation of why I like each one. Matt can offer his thoughts on my choices, and even offer alternatives when he considers my taste to be, well, how can I put this? Piss-poor. With half a loaf-ful of trepidation and a rumbled Bronx-ful of enthusiasm, I present (in no particular order) my ten choices, and Matt's reactions to them.

Magnificent Bodyguards (1978, Thai variant)

AD: There are several reasons I like this. Firstly, it's landscape. How many posters do you get that are landscape? And before you mention your precious British quads, I mean 'landscape and not the size of the Bayeux Tapestry'. You could frame it without having to steal the side of a bus shelter. Secondly, the hand-drawn artwork is mint. It's an all-action, kinetic, weapon-filled montage of scenes from the movie, all painted in the individual style of a top artist (whoever that is – it's hard to find information on that!). There's no lazy photographs plastered on there. It's just a crazily energetic piece of work. Finally, I just can't get past that black border. It's like the artist said, 'I've used a paintbox-full of colours here. How to I maintain the integrity of them, without swamping them.' And he's only gone and done it! It's brilliant. I dare you to argue against me on that one!

MR: Absolutely love this poster, it's one of my faves. The artwork is slightly similar to the rare Hong Kong landscape version, but on this one the colours are much more vivid and striking to the eye. As per usual with Thai movie posters, the hand drawn artwork is top notch, and as Alan points out, it's a landscape version. It's down to personal preference, but visually I always prefer landscape versions of posters, and this particular one uses it to great advantage. So, no arguments on this one, it's top drawer!

AD: You mean this one? I've never seen

that one in the wild. In fact, and I'll level with you here, I've never seen it before, full stop. Shame, shame, shame, etc. It's a little belter. To be honest, it momentarily caused me to reassess the primacy of the Thai effort. On reflection, I still prefer that one, but this HK one is spectacularly good.

MR: Both are superb to be fair. Love the way the leg on the left of the poster is short and stubby on the Thai version, compared to the extraordinarily long leg on the Hong Kong version. Definitely had a leg extension there. Think those feet are size 12s, minimum. Good luck searching for these two super examples of 1970s kung fu movie poster artwork!

Eagle's Shadow (1978, US variant)

AD: Let's take a look at this doozy. You know I don't have much love for US posters in general, but this one is different. It's got such style! I think the art is by Neal Adams, and you can tell that he's spent a lot of time and effort fashioning a design that is both striking and powerful. The co-stars are beautifully drawn. Look at Roy Horan. It's like something Kung Fu Bob would produce. The swooping lines scything from top to bottom add a visceral quality – even down to the red lines smudged above and below Jackie's name. Talking of which … urgh. No. I know it was his 'name' at one point, but there's something about the 'y' that just looks plain wrong. You can probably enlighten me a bit more on this point, Matt. What a unique poster, though! Top rank!

MR: One of the first Jackie films I ever saw, and also one of the first images I ever saw when I rented the old Rank video VHS from my local video store, under the real title 'Snake in the Eagle's Shadow.' For me, this is a super-iconic poster, not only because it spells Jackie's name slightly wrong, but because it remains in

my head as one of the foremost images that ignited my love of Hong Kong movies. Obviously, I prefer the Hong Kong version. But this one sits very highly with me. It must do because I put it in a frame! The artwork is a nice montage of scenes from the film clustered together in the middle section, with the large

eagle taking centre stage in the middle, surrounding what can only be described as an 'artist's impression' of Jackie. An iconic image and one of the best martial arts films of all time!

AD: Thinking about the HK poster, the US variant is massively different. You'd barely equate it with the same film when you compare the images. See, this is where you have an advantage over me. I didn't get into these movies until the 2000s. You grew up through the VHS era, with all the excitement of new releases busting your wallet every week. These posters have more of an emotional connection for you. Regrettably, I'm quite jealous of it!

MR: Finally, age has its advantages then, Alan. I would like to point out that the Japanese poster has some very - and I mean, very - bizarre artwork for this movie. A very cartoon Jackie is being groped by a sexy blonde lady, as a giant snake surrounds them. Personally, I find the font used on the overseas versions super-iconic, and was pleased that 88 Films continued the font theme in their recent UK Blu-ray release of the movie. Fantastico!

Shaolin Wooden Men (1976, Japanese variant)

AD: OK. Moving on, what do you think of this? I generally like Japanese posters, especially the Bruce Lee ones. A lot of Jackie's, though, are very busy. Too busy for my tastes. This one, however, is crisp and to the point. It evokes the Fist of Fury poster where Bruce's face takes up a massive portion of the design. You can see the raw emotion in Jackie's expression. What is that emotion? Anger? Desperation? A cry of vengeance? The viewer is left pondering the tone of the film. It's an eye-catching, punter-hooking image. The other parts of the poster show Jackie in a classic fighting pose, and there's a couple of action scenes at the top. The red slash from the top left is stunning, and suggests bloodshed. The fonts are clear and unfussy. It's a neat poster, and not infested with the garishness of some of the other designs to emerge from Japan.

MR: Okay, so I will keep this simple. I really don't like this poster. Which is extremely unusual for me to say, because generally Japan knocks posters out of the park when it comes to design! I love Jackie's raw, battle cry face on the left, but the image on the bottom right, a stagnant studio shot of Jackie, kind of ruins the poster. The images in the top left don't really sell the film either. My favourite poster for this film has to be the Hong Kong version, but I still think a there's cracking artwork still to be done for this movie. Artists at the ready!

AD: Are you kidding? The only thing the HK poster does better is the black and white figures in the background. The rest isn't all that much better! Are the images at the foot of the poster really an improvement? Furthermore, Jackie looks confident and powerful in the action shot, which changes the dynamics of what the film promises. The poster is one big advert, really, and these two variants seem to suggest very different things tonally.

MR: You win.

AD: Obviously, you don't really mean that…

MR: Nah.

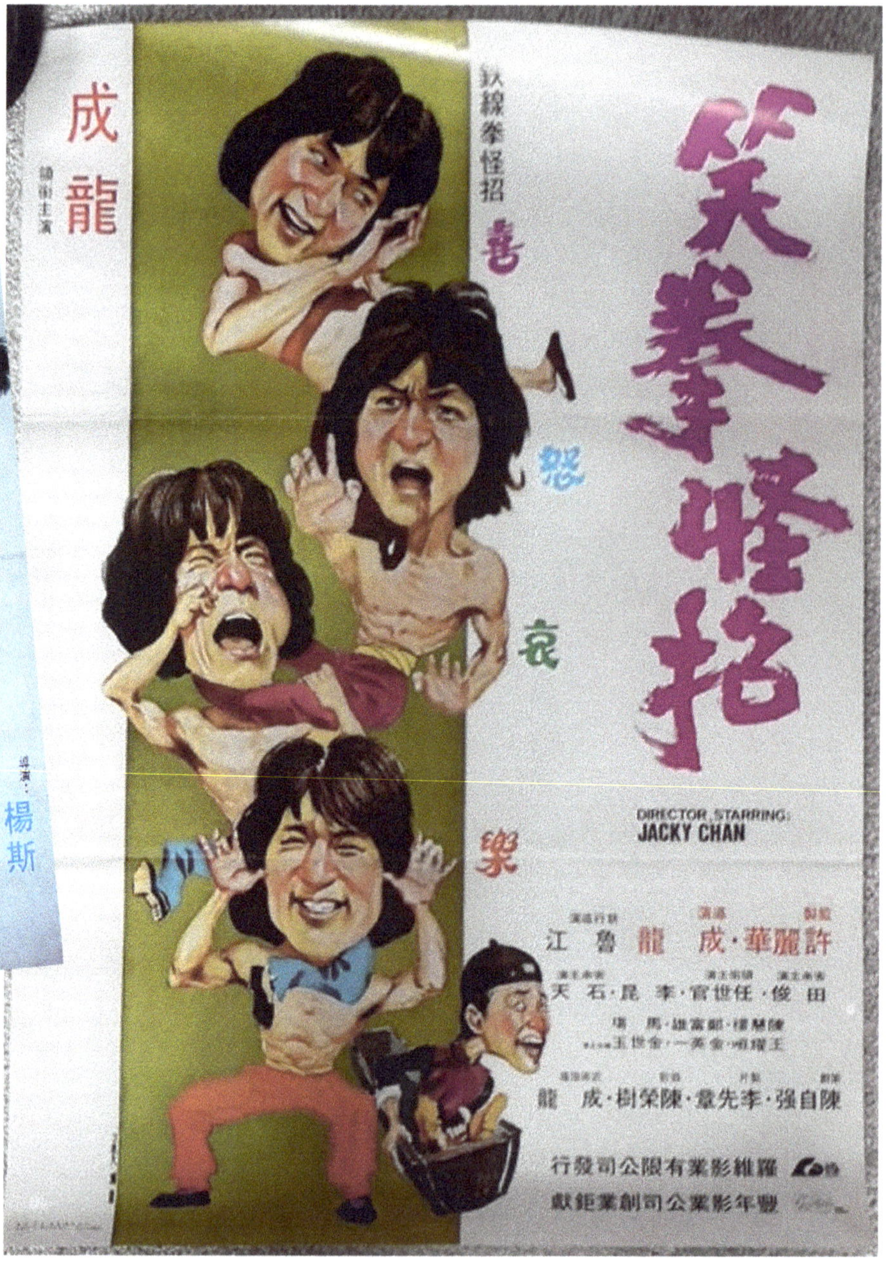

Fearless Hyena (1979, HK variant)

AD: Bit of a leftfield choice, this one. Cartoons on film posters are very hit and miss for me, and at first glance, this was no exception. It just feels like the four Jackie images suggest a lot of arsing around. I mean, look at them, for crying out loud. A wailing Jackie with a red nose, like the most annoying characters from a Korean Elton Chong/Dragon Lee kung fu comedy. God save us. It's almost genre code for 'unwatchable, cringeworthy dross.' Then the bottom image of Jackie acting like a child. It hardly entices the viewer. I had these views for quite a while. Then something changed, and I can't pinpoint when or why. Perhaps I temporarily shelved my curmudgeonly outlook. Whatever the reason, one day I looked at the poster and smiled. It's a rather lovely summary of the character's emotional journey. The pictures are beautifully-sketched and that gold band really sparkles behind the star. There's something pure and simple about the poster, and I'm glad to have discovered its charms, no matter how late I was to the party.

MR: One of my personal fave Jackie movies. I actually love the original Transglobal VHS Video cover art from the UK release in the mid-1980s. It depicts Jackie in the end fight in full-on gritty, muscle tensed, battle-scarred glory. This poster is a lot of fun, with nicely drawn cartoon images that show the stages Jackie's character goes through in this movie's unique 'Hyena' fighting style. The poster is very 'of its time' and could arguably be a pre-cursor to a siege of similar 'cartoon-esque' Hong Kong poster artwork that was to grace the 1980s (this film being from around 1979). For me, the poster has a lot of character and is definitely worthy of being in your Jackie collection!

AD: I know what you mean about the cartoony efforts. They always seemed to follow the same format: a few figures on a white background. I'm looking at you, Bolo! And Kung Fu Warrior! And Taoism Drunkard! Etc. Would Drunken Master be an earlier pacesetter in this regard?

Dragon Lord (1982, HK variant)

AD: Cards on the table. I love this one. Again, the stark white background does a tremendous job in thrusting the photos into the foreground. At face value, I should hate those random panels spread around. They look like one of those trendy wall-art displays you get in Ikea, with a single image fractured into sections. I don't 'do' trendy, but this looks bloody fantastic. Jackie looks great, too, belting a thirty yard screamer into the top corner. The arrangement of text is really compact and ordered. This is one of those posters that looks even better in real life. The dozens of white-shirted seem to buzz with energy, suggesting an action-packed extravaganza for the dedicated fan and curious punter alike. What say you, Mr Routledge?

MR: Ahhh, the shuttlecock sequence! After doing the rumoured 1500 takes to get it right, I can easily see why Jackie might want to have that as the main image on the poste. It's a typical, great, mid-action shot of Jackie. The type I used to try to emulate both when I was a kid, and also when I actually had that much hair! I love the yellow writing. and the beginning of the 80s style of showing mini character pictures dotted around the poster. This time, they're used to compliment the tower on the right-hand side of the image. It's a simple and effective design from one very fun Jackie movie!

AD: Please tell me you have photos of these attempts!

MR: It would be great if somehow the Golden Harvest archive could release an unedited reel of the rushes, to see just how many takes there were, but sadly I think that might never happen. Onto the next lovely poster.

The Killer Meteors (1976, Korean variant)

AD: Well, it certainly is lovely. It's hand-drawn. That's always a winner in my book. The one thing that doesn't work for me is the massive face in the top left. It's a good drawing, but I just don't like it. I guess it's meant to showcase a profound, pensive expression, but to me it just looks like a face painted on a balloon. The rest is great, even down to the ridiculous title. 'The Cometic Sword' – what does that even mean? The scene at the foot of the poster is the best one as far as I'm concerned. It's serene, elegant, and oozes 'wuxia'. It's straight from a Ku Long novel. It's also the least 'kung fu' image on the whole poster. The colours are rather washed out, but that's probably down to age, and the atrocious quality of the paper that Korean posters in this era were printed on.

MR: I know Wang Yu divides opinion in martial arts movie circles, but I personally love him. This is a nice poster, and I don't actually think that the image in the top left is that bad, it's just that you know there is probably a much better action-style image that they could have used instead. The red letters are striking and eye catching, with a terrific image of Wang Yu holding the spear to the right centre. But here is my big problem with this poster: the images are from 'Blood of the Dragon,' a 1971 film, 5 years before 'Killer Meteors', and Wang is sporting a beard. I usually totally can't stand posters that pinch artwork from other films, with the rare exceptions being the Jackie VPD UK VHS releases of 'Twinkle Twinkle Lucky Stars' and 'Dragons Forever.' A decent poster, but let's get on to the one that is way better.

AD: I genuinely didn't know that the images were ripped from a different film. The QI-style klaxon is sounding, with the words 'IDIOT ALERT' loud and proud behind me.

MR: Right, Alan, for not knowing

that, you have to sell me all of your Jimmy Wang Yu posters, effective immediately, for not being a true fan! Or, alternatively, you can show me your iron palm technique by submerging your hands in a bucket of hot stones. Your choice.

AD: I'll do the latter. I can't let those post-ers go. I can still enjoy looking at my posters - it'll just make it a little trickier using charred stumps to flick between them.

The Killer Meteors (1976, HK variant)

AD: Can I sense a raised eyebrow? Yeah, yeah. It's the same film. Could you tell that, though? If I hadn't said? This is a totally different visual representation of the Jimmy Wang Yu-starring flick. Everything about the poster stands out. I defy anyone to say it's not a 'worldie', as the young 'uns say. It's hand-drawn, again, and lacking any balloon bonces. The characters are aggressive and brooding. Tonally, the vibe of the image is far darker and more explosive. The blood red text, the smudged chaos, the flashes of yellow – brilliant! It's a poster that promises much, which is what a poster is designed to do. Even the lighter sections look dark. This is a top-level Jackie poster, Matt.

MR: Holy moly, this one is a cracker. A brilliant, hand drawn, colourful, stunning montage that sells a bang-on average film into something way bigger and better. This is what posters should always do: elevate the film, make you want to see the film and catch your eye. This one has all that in spades. Totally agree with you on this one - stunning artwork, and I'd buy that for a dollar, although quite likely this one would cost way more than a dollar!

AD: Ahem. Possibly. People pay stupid money for things this good, or so I've heard. Did your hair used to be that long, too? Find a photo, and we can photoshop a bandana with a garish gemstone onto your forehead. What did you say again? Digital artists at the ready!

MR: Happy to provide said photograph, as I am sure Ricky will put it on the front cover on the next issue. Great idea Alan!

Snake in the Eagle's Shadow (1978, Thai variant)

AD: There are actually two posters for this film in Thailand. One is in portrait format and presents Jackie in the classic SITES stance, with an arm-blur effect to showcase the transition into snake fist. I quite like it, but I gather that some people feel that it looks a bit cheap, so it's a bit of a marmite image. Regardless, I prefer this variant. The central image of Jackie and Yuen Siu-tien, snake fists locked inside a hoop, setting sun between them, should be more iconic than it seems to be. It shows the master and his student, working hard to prepare for battle against a deadly foe. The action/training sketches dotted around, bleached in different hues using oils and acrylics, are sensitively and skillfully drawn and shaded. It's another example of 1970s-era Thai theatrical poster greatness.

MR: A beautiful poster - a classic Thai 1970s-style impression of some of the most iconic scenes in the movie, drawn by Thai movie poster legend 'Uncle'. I really do love the Thai poster artwork. The pictures are always seem to be blended into each other with breathtaking skill and effect. This has the edge over the USA version in terms of hand drawn imagery, but not in terms of iconic-ness (if that even is a word). My favourite poster for the film will always be the Hong Kong version, but this really is a cracker, and should definitely be in anyone's Jackie poster collection. There is a Thai version that is vertical, which is also a beauty and depicts Jackie solo, holding the Snake form, but I personally prefer this landscape version. Nice one, Uncle!

AD: What do you make of that concertina fist movement image? There's just something about it that, for me, is cheesier than a Ricky Baker chat-up line.

MR: Rick hasn't tried a chat up line on me yet - you have obviously been way luckier than me in that department. Either way, two smashing examples of artwork for this all-time classic Jackie movie!

Miracles (1989, HK variant)

AD: Mr Routledge requires medical assistance! He seems to have fainted in shock. Anyone got any smelling salts? Yeah, yeah, I picked the poster of a 'modern' film. Ok, it's not exactly a 'modern', but it's after 1985, so well outside my shapes-and-bashers comfort zone. The drawings on this poster aren't particularly remarkable in a stylistic sense. They are just photo-like sketches. What I really like about this piece are the little touches. The gun and the rose in the title, for example. The sepia flush of the parade of characters at the bottom of the poster, reflecting its pre-war period setting. The rose-print upper background. And, of course, the centrepiece: a tommy gun stood in the most bizarre pose, dividing the two leads. It's a cracker.

MR: I can't believe you picked a modern film, Alan! This is at least 10 years out of your domain. You must definitely be on the smelling salts! On to the poster - it's lovely. The movie is set in the 1930s, and this poster almost tries to emulate an old-style design from that era. Colours are subtle, yet perfectly balanced. There's pinks and reds, with two lovely, hand-drawn character pieces for Jackie and Anita Mui sitting in the centre. I have to say this is one of my favourite posters for 'Miracles', along with Kung Fu Bob's great artwork on the recent 88 Films blu-ray edition, released here in the UK.

AD: I keep expecting Jackie to down tools and start judging pineapples. That hat, man! It seems that we both say 'yes' to this one!
MR: Yes :-)

New Fist of Fury (1976, HK variant)

AD: I don't want any arguments about this one! It's in the classic tradition of early 1970s Taiwanese posters, with an action pose dominating the scene, and an assortment of faces dotted around. There's so much to admire. Look at the way the star is bordered in a white motion blur, caused by the power of the kick. See how the same white lines are used to map the movement of the arm and fist. Look at the energy in the pose – every muscle is taut and bulging, and the kick strong and true. Observe the three different background colours that blend seamlessly. Finally, the title text. That chunky black border for each character is absolutely stunning. This is poster design at its best.

MR: Sheer awesomeness on every level. A poster that is much better than the actual film. The red lettering at the bottom really catches the eye but it's Jackie's high kick and ripped torso that dominates. It's a slightly similar concept to part one, with Bruce doing a flying kick stealing the show, but you just can't beat the 70s hand drawn artwork. The characters and expressions are always beautifully captured. The colours are, yet again, very striking, with red playing a large part in this particular design. A very rare poster to obtain for collectors, but an absolute must if you are lucky enough to get the opportunity!

AD: Another consensus! I like the parallel you've drawn with the original film. It is, as you say, a striking image.

MR: Looking at it again, I might bring Jackie's foot down a smidgen, but it does look like they have done it on purpose so that it looks like his outstretched foot is touching the top of the paper. Still awesome!

AD: Well, I'm surprised that our tastes tallied so well! Apart from one bone of contention (which you're obviously wrong about). Are there any other Jackie posters that you think could be jostling for position in this top ten? I've considered that Spiritual Kung Fu might get a look in, with its primary colours on an action-packed background. I'm just not sold on the reflection at the top, or the

'Jacky'spelling.

MR: Definitely. The 1980s VPD Quad Poster for 'Armour of God' has sublime artwork and is a terrific design in its own right, as is the international one sheet poster, which is very hard to come by these days. I do also have a soft spot for the French Grande version named 'Mr Dynamite.' It's blooming huge, but very striking, colourful and fun. The French Grande version of 'Dragons Forever' is also a cartoon art cracker.
Further honourable mentions must go to the two Hong Kong variants for 'Battle Creek Brawl,' that boast super cartoon montage artwork too, but honestly, I could keep on naming more and more titles. It would be interesting to do a poll here to see which are everyone else's favourites. Anyway, enough from me, Alan's ranting on is contagious. Keep watching those kung fu flicks folks!!

AD: Cheers, Matt. Great insights throughout. I'm off to double the security detail on my collection.

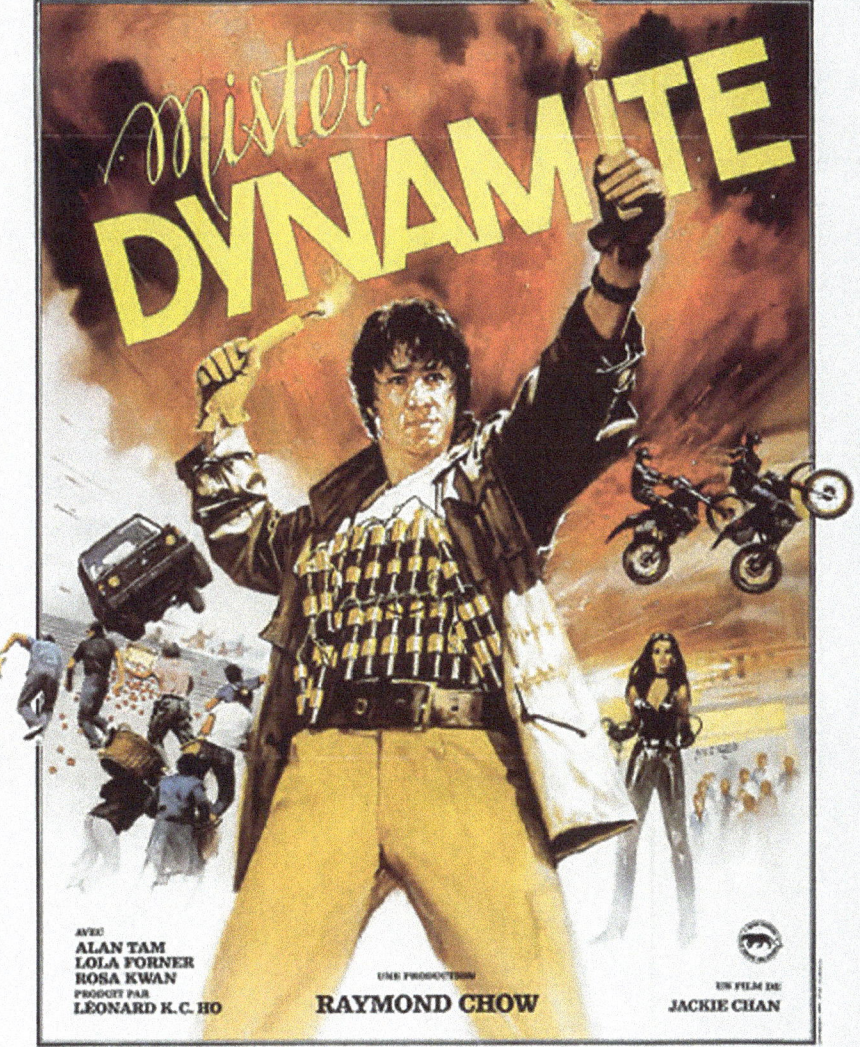
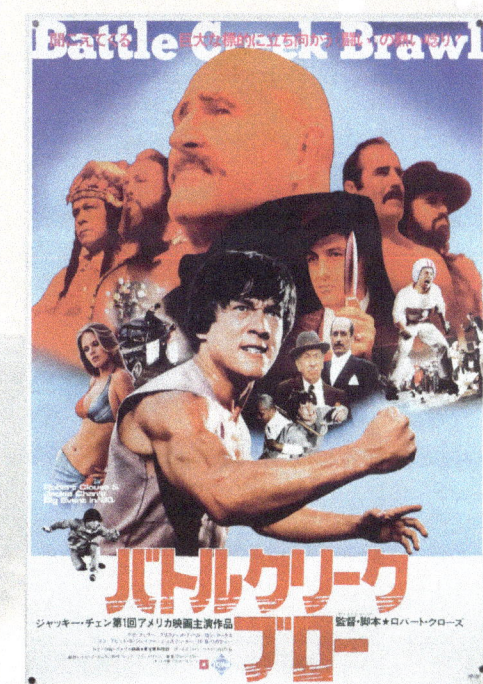

Dragons Forever poster designed by Tim Hollingsworth for the Jackie Chan Appreciation Group

FANATICAL DRAGON PRESENTS
5 FINGERS OF DISCS
FULL METAL JACKIE

Way back in issue #1 I gave a list of 5 of the best Jackie Chan Bluray releases currently available, in the ensuing months we've had one long awaited new kid on the block fight it's way into the rankings, 88 Films' release of Jackie Chan's Armour of God was a Bluray treat we'd waited long for and it absolutely delivered, let's dive into the release below and what better time to also take a look at the series of movies it kick started… Operation Condor and Chinese Zodiac CZ12.

In a tip of the hat to our cover star Brett Ratner, I also take a quick look at the best edition of his Rush Hour trilogy available anywhere just now, the US Mondo Edition. We look ahead to Cine-Asia's upcoming release of Benny Chan's final film, the Donnie Yen
Hk Crime thriller Raging Fire. I also take a look forward to a few of the other new titles we have to coming up in Twenty Twenty Two.

Palm-Flick-fu your chewing gum into your mouths and let's get into it.

Armour of God (1986)

88 Films Deluxe Edition
Dir - Jackie Chan
REG B

Armour of God, one of the JC films most direly in need of a makeover and a decent release finally got it's time to shine late last year thanks to the immense efforts of the mighty warriors over at 88 Films who have delivered a truly incredible set. I'm sure a large number of you found under your Xmas tree this year (giving to yourself still counts as giving right? Yep, totally still counts)

Quite possibly the best Deluxe release from the company so far, managing even to top the seller work they did in 2021 on their other Deluxe editions for The Young Master, Riki-Oh, Robotric and Erotic Ghost Story. Yes indeed, Jackie Chan's Armour of God arrived in all it's full deluxe edition glory just in time to shake up the winter releases, pausing to give Arrow's year stealing Shawscope Volume 1 Boxset a dirty look, crack open a beer and flash it's multiple commentary tracks at it. I always feel I'm preaching to the choir somewhat telling you guys about movies I'm confident we've all seen countless times, but can't help keeping in mind Stan Lee's old adage about every Spider-man comic being somebody's FIRST spider-man comic, so for any amongst you who many not know the movie…

Armour of God is a 1986 action adventure movie written, directed and starring Jackie Chan. Created after the actor/director/producer/tv host/TVB Head Honcho Eric Tsang's suggestion that they produce an 'Asian Indiana Jones' movie.. Jackie would go on to play the character of 'Asian Hawk' aka 'Martin' and eventually just 'JC' as the series progressed through it's three various outings. Another in the fairly long line of JC movies filmed primarily outside of HK, production in this case took place in what was at the time, Yugoslavia as well as filming in Spain, France and Morocco.

The franchise would showcase globetrotting locations, and usually present Jackie working as part of a small group to find a missing person or lost treasure, sometimes both, as is the case in the original movie.

Overall they're excellent movies, maybe not as well loved or as well regarded as the Police Story films by critics outside of the JC/Kung Fu/East Asian Cinema communities, but ask any of the thousands of JC and HK cinema fans who do love these movies and they'll all tell you the same thing in a Police Story Vs Armour of God debate: The Armour of God series is way more fun. This first film in the series is much more rough and tumble than its slicker, bigger budget sequels, Operation Condor and CZ12/Chinese Zodiac, but some of its set pieces hit just as hard, maybe even harder in a few instances. Its final reel especially has some of the fiercest Jackie Vs a small group hand to hand fighting we would ever see from the star, we're all thinking of the Jackie Vs Amazonian fighters here. And as you all also will likely know, Armour of God carries with it the legacy of being the movie that very nearly killed Chan, after a relatively small stunt jumping from a wall to a tree ('small' in JC terms, it would be instant death for me I'm sure) went horribly wrong, and resulted in Jackie having a steel plate fitted to his skull. The troubled production along with the enormous entertainment factor of the movie itself allows for a deep dive into the film and it's star in the presentation and production of the package of extras that 88 have put together for the movie. It really is a beast of a set, easily 88's best overall packaged and stacked Asia Collection release since The Young Master (which they released early in 2021), they've outdone themselves in terms of extras this time around, and given the film's fascinating place in JC's filmography, that it was the movie that very nearly killed him makes this a title so worthy of a decent edition that could do a deep dive into the movie and its production and deep dive they do..A new 4K remaster of the HK theatrical cut of the movie with multiple audio options, 4 x Cantonese and 2 x English audio options offering up the 'Lorelei and Flight of the Dragon' versions of the movie along with two new 'hybrid' Cantonese/English tracks.

Three excellent audio commentary tracks, one from the Master of Remaster himself Frank Djeng, as loaded and information packed a track as I've ever heard from him (\ which is saying something, his tracks are always tightly scripted and finely tuned to pack in as much info as possible, Frank must do some serious homework for these!)

The second track is from 88 films regulars, Big Mike Leeder and Arne Venema, giving us a more light hearted track with that great sense of just hanging out with mates down the pub chatting movies. The Third track is from Kenneth Brorsson and Phil Gillon of the Podcast On Fire Network, which I must confess I've not dived into yet, but I will, as I've heard many episodes of their podcast, and excited to hear their take on the movie too. Scott Adkins recorded special episode of his Art of Action series for the set, working as a video commentary to the key action sequences in the movie as Scott and Matt Routledge break down the shots and sequences, the stand-ins and the painfuls, its a great idea for an extra!

Extremely excited to see another episode of the HK TV Show Celebrity Talk Show in full presented on the set, I have no idea how many episodes of the show 88 have access to, but I hope we get one of these with every Deluxe release, they're so great to see subbed and in full.

(you can find another full episode on 88's release of Erotic Ghost Story). We also get a stack of music videos, interviews and trailers, 6 replica lobby cards and 88's finest book to date, it features a marvellous article on Eastern Heroes by Tim Murray inside it (Maybe I'm a little biased) alongside the Eastern Heroes love, is a great piece titled 'Jackie Chan, a trademark designed to succeed' by Thorsten Boose and followed up by

It's quite simply, a truly quality, definitive and loving presentation that the film has long deserved.

Pixelated Punch: The Early Video Game Years of Jackie Chan by Audi Sorlie plus an Interview with Thorsten Nickel. The shorter international cut of the movie is presented on a second disc.

Armour of God 2 - Operation Condor (1991)
88 Films
Dir - Jackie Chan
REG - B

Faster, bigger, more bombastic and much slicker than it's predecessor, Operation Condor is early 90's Jackie in his globetrotting action/comedy/adventure mode at its finest, this time around on the hunt for lost Nazi Gold in the heart of the desert. The set pieces are bigger, the jokes come way faster and more frequently

We've had a decent release for Operation Condor in the UK for quite some time now, 88 films put this out a while before they introduced their 'Deluxe' format, and in light of the new release of the first Armour of God, I do wonder if 88 films will revisit Operation Condor and pimp up this edition of it a little, that being said though, their existing bluray is fantastic.

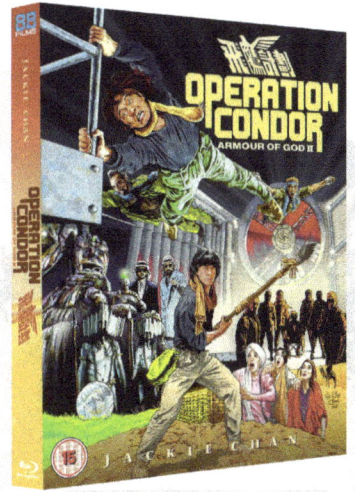

They give us a 2K Remaster from The Original 35mm Negative of a never-before-seen Extended Version of the movie [117 mins approx] in Cantonese Mono as well as a 2K restoration of the Original Hong Kong Version [107 mins approx] we get both Cantonese and classic English Dub options on both.

Whilst not nearly as loaded as Armour of God there's absolutely enough on there to keep you entertained long after the movie credits have played. Most notably the Mike Leeder and Arne Venema commentary track, which I tend to listen to more often than the movie audio when i watch it these days, is the lad's usual laugh along mix of banter and brain food, offering up facts and jokes in equal measure.

We also get an interview with actor Bruce Fontaine, trailers and if you're lucky enough to track down a copy of the Bluray with the original booklet, inside you'll find a great article titled Go Go Asian Hawk: The Gadgets and adventures of an international super explorer by William Blaik, an interview with lead stuntman Vincent Lyn along with images showing behind the scenes shots, the original lobby cards and promo posters for the movie all presented alongside some more wonderful Kung Fu Bob O'Brien sketches.

Armour of God 3 - CZ12 aka Chinese Zodiac (2012)
Nova Media
Dir - Jackie Chan
REG - FREE

Ok, I know, this one isn't going to win first place in anyone's favourite JC movie, but I do actually have a soft spot for CZ12 amongst the more recent Jackie Chan movies. It's a far better ensemble movie than Vanguard and a much more coherent a film overall than Bleeding Steel.
It's not up to the dizzying heights of the other two movies in the AOG series, but I do find myself returning to it quite often, it's a great Sunday afternoon, easy going adventure story. Jackie and his team on the search for Stolen Antiques, in this instance, 12 statue heads depicting the 12 different animal characters in the Chinese Zodiac. Jackie and his gang of hi-tech, morally questionable, international (thieves?) treasure hunters tasked with finding the statues and delivering them for auction…

The action sequences are growing ever more CG assisted, but at the movie's core here are still a great many nods to classic era Jackie Chan stunt team hijinks. Well, I dig it anyway ;)

There is a UK release of Chinese Zodiac easily available but I wanted to share this Korean edition of the movie with you all here, It's pretty reasonably priced and comes with much nicer artwork and a Digibook style case.

Rush Hour Trilogy (1998 - 2007)

Mondo 5 Disc Limited Edition Set.
Dir - Brett Ratner
REG - PART REGION FREE, PART REG A

It's often easy for us old gits to forget, but for a huge number of people, especially those in the USA and particularly those under the age of 30, the Rush Hour movies were often their first introduction to Jackie Chan. To a whole generation of fans who had never encountered any HK cinema before, these movies were a gateway to dive into Jackie's back catalogue and beyond.

The three films may not gather the same praise and adulation as Jackie's Hong Kong movies, but they are far and away his most successful live action American films in financial terms and continue to retain a legion of devoted fans. The series often managed to bring in some

truly surprising guest stars into the films over the years, Zhang Ziyi, Don Cheadle, Max Von Sydow, Hiroyuki Sanada and even Roman Polanski all appeared in the movies alongside Jackie Chan and Chris Tucker.

We've never really had a decent trilogy release of the movies on Bluray here in the UK, (1 and 3 are available individually), but there is a really nice 5 disc trilogy boxset available stateside which oddly is almost directly accessible for UK fans even if they don't have a multi region Bluray player.
In the US 5 disc set, only the two Rush Hour 3 discs for are Region A (US region coded) all the other discs on the set will play fine in any UK Bluray player or Bluray games console. And you can easily pick up a standalone release of RH3 and swap the discs.

The US set with it's excellent Mondo produced cover art, is stacked with extras across all three movies as well as a standalone disc created for the set with Brett Ratner and Jackie Chan looking back at the three movies. Ratner also provides a commentary track for each movie, we also get deleted scenes, behind the scenes and a featurette gallery.

Raging Fire (2021)

Cine Asia UK Steelbook
Dir - Benny Chan
REG - B

One of the cinematic highlights for us in 2021 was getting a chance to view Benny Chan's final movie Raging Fire on the big screen, as much as I adore physical media, you can't beat seeing a movie for the first time at the cinema and thanks to Cine Asia taking the movie out into UK cinemas for a limited run many of us got the chance to see this excellent slice of HK crime drama,
quite a throwback or love note to the HK action movies we all adored in the 80's 90's and 00's.

Donnie Yen and Nicolas Tse playing two cops, former colleagues, now facing off against each other in a really well directed, well produced, beautifully shot and extremely well staged action thriller. Cine

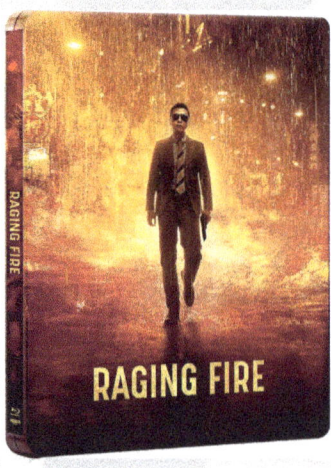

Asia have the film coming out in the UK on Bluray on January 31st, and whilst I wasn't able to get my hands on a copy before we went to print, there is a rather nice dual format Bluray/4K UHD steelbook release being offered via Zavvi. I don't always go down the 4K or steelbook routes, but I really enjoyed the movie and want to support Cine Asia in their future releases. Their Bluray release of the great wee Korean Martial Arts movie The Swordsman was my sleeper hit of 2021.

In the case of their Raging Fire release, we get six behind the scenes featurettes on the Bluray and separate behind the scenes footage exclusive to the UHD disc, there is also a 12 page booklet with contributions from Mike Leeder, Daniel Wu, Mike Fury, Ben Johnson, Ken Law, Andy On, Philip Ng and star Donnie Yen.

The film was a really welcome return, (hopefully not a swan song) to the type of movie that HK used to be so damn good at making, to the cop vs gangster thriller's that still captivate so many of us today, to the Better Tomorrow's, the Infernal Affairs, The Young and yes indeed, The Dangerous, it remains as a glorious, high note to bring Benny Chan's long and starred career to a close.

Coming up in 2022!

From our good friends over at 88 Films comes a Deluxe edition of the HK Cat3 Thriller Black Cat due to release in Feb as will two Shaw Brother's epics, Flag of Iron and Legendary Weapons of China. March brings more Shaw Brother's, Lau Kar Leung's Shaolin Mantis and Monkey Kung Fu with Human Lanterns, Martial Club, Chuck Norris's Good Guys Wear Black and… Jackie Chan's Half a Loaf of Kung Fu all due for later in the year.

Yuen Biao and Sammo Hung fans rejoice for Eureka are bringing out Bluray editions of the Wing Chun masterpieces The Prodigal Son and Warriors Two in a double feature release in Jan followed by individual, standalone releases for Sammo Hung/Lau Kar Wing classic The Odd Couple in Feb and The Sammo/Karl Maka comedy-fu Skinny Tiger, Fatty Dragon in March. Eureka have also teased out images promising releases of Shaolin Plot, Dreadnaught and Hapkido all set for release throughout 2022.

We also have Arrow's Shawscope Volume 2 boxset now due seemingly in June and now confirmed to include: My Young Auntie, Invincible Shaolin, 10 Tigers from Kwantung, The Kid With The Golden Arm and Magnificent Ruffians and heavily rumoured to include The 36th Chamber of Shaolin and it's sequel Return to the 36th Chamber, yet more rumours indicate a standalone release of the Lau Kar Leung epic, time will tell. Facts will follow. Arrow have definitively announced a standalone release of King Hu's seminal Wu Xia movie Come Drink With Me, releasing as a US/Region A only version in March. This is one of two standalone Shaw's titles Arrow have coming out in 2022 in addition to the boxset. I believe both standalone titles will be Region A. The Boxset will be worldwide.

You can expect to see at least one HK or East Asian Bluray release from Eureka or 88 films every month in 2022, it's somewhat of a golden age to be a collector of HK and East Asian Cinema, albeit a very expensive one.

You can be absolutely sure we'll be reviewing all the very best of them right here, see you all in Issue #4

COMPETITION TIME!

Thanks once again to the incredible generosity of the Bluray sifu's over at 88 films,
We have one Deluxe Edition of Armour or God to give away to one lucky reader.
To enter simply send a photo of yourself with your copy of this issue of the magazine
(or alongside all your Eastern Heroes Issues if you have more!)
And email it over to us at: easternheroescompetition@gmail.com
The competition will run until the 3rd March.

Good Luck to all who enter!

Lastly, HUGE Congratulations to reader **Shaun Long** who won our 88 Films Dragon Forever Steelbook competition which launched in issue 3.

www.youtube.com/thefanaticaldragon

THAT CONDOR MOMENT

An Interview with Vincent Lyn
By Rick Baker

For this special Jackie Chan issue, I wanted to talk to a few people that had worked with Jackie on film projects. In this interview I caught with an old Friend Vincent Lyn who had the pleasure of working on Jackie on his Smash hit "Armour of God 2"

Vincent Lyn Mini Bio
Forever winning in Chinese is Yong Sheng. Vincent Lyn was born to a Chinese father and a British mother. His English name is Sir Vincent Raymond Percival Lyn. Vincent is the kind of individual whom you instinctively know when you meet him that he is someone worth finding out more about and the more you peel away layers of the onion, the more impressed you'll be. He speaks in a soft voice with remnants of a British accent. He was born in Yemen as his father was stationed there with the British Royal Air Force. At two years old Vincent and his family moved to Ethiopia, Khartoum (Sudan), Algeria, Netherlands, then England. He emigrated to the United States at age 16 and then to Hong Kong after his university studies. Not coincidently, Vincent's multi-linguistic son, who is also a recent USA university graduate, now lives in Hong Kong. if you look up the definition of a Renaissance man, you may very well see a photo of Vincent, His talents, abilities, skills and interests are far-reaching and as diversified as anyone you'll ever meet. In the following paragraphs are a summary of a few of his many accomplishments as they are truly vast and impressive.

I first met Vincent back in the 80's when he attended an event in Birmingham, for a few short moments I thought he might become my new step dad as my mum exclaiming "what a lovely looking young man" attempted do snuggle up to him and kiss him and saying " oh I want to take him home". He was the perfect gentleman, and he did not call

the police as I rescued him from her clutches and it was all taken tongue in cheek. Luckily years later and my Kung Fu fan mum now passed away, Vincent obviously felt safe to talk me via Zoom (Smile)

I started by asking Vincent for a few experiences working with Jackie on A.O.G.2.

VL - Well there is a lot (takes deep breath) I will start for the beginning. Originally when they cast the film they basically took on every gweilo (common Cantonese slur term for Westerners). Actually, even though I auditioned along with everybody else I was not initially chosen there were two of us left myself and Mark Houghton. I actually did not join the set until about six months later, by that stage Jackie had now got rid of the original script idea and was writing it himself with Edward Tang and they auditioned again. Originally I was only signed for a ten day contract, but actually I spent the first 10 days in make-up.

RB – So where did you have to go to film, did you go to the dessert location?

VL – No, My scenes were filmed up at the Shaw Brothers Studio when they rebuilt the whole wind tunnel set, so there I am spending the first 10 days in make-up and Jackie would come down to see how my make-up looked. He would peak his head around the corner and say "No good! Start it again). He wanted the make-up artist to make me more Ugly (laughs) because in his words "he is to good looking to be a villain" So you know, keep having my make-up done and all of a sudden my ten day contract is over. So I had to sign a new contract, but I said listen rather than sign a new contract would it not be better for me to just show up every day? And then just pay me at the end of each day.

RB – How did that work out for you?

VL – Well it was actually a smart thing on my part because it went on for months and months

RB – Sounds like the dream job (Laughs) so what happened next?

VL – well one day I see Wang Yu peer his head around the corner and Jackie kind of stands to attention and goes over to talk to him. When he comes back he said "Vincent do you know who that guy was?" and I replied "I do not recognise him" Jackie says "remember that movie the One armed Boxer" I said "Yes One Armed boxer, I used to love watching his films even before Bruce lee" and he replied "You know who he is now!" I said "Erm Nope!" he said "Big triad Boss"

RB – Yes, I believe a long time ago he ripped Jackie's contract up with Lo Wei so he could go film I think it was Drunken master with Ng see Yuen. But! Later down the line that act did not come without favours, because when Jimmy wanted to make "Island on Fire" he made Jackie, Sammo and Andy Lau star in it and if the story is true, FOR FREE!. So you can see the hold that he still has over Jackie.

VL – Really, you know I met Wang Yu four or five years ago in New York City at the Lincoln centre receiving a life time achievement reward. He was much older and a little frailer and maybe a little more subdued, but it was nice to see him again after all those years.

RB – Ok so back to the set

VL – well I was spending up to three hours every day in make-up and it was becoming hard work you know, having

to do these stunts flying around in this heavy make-up was the most uncomfortable experience. Some days I would be sitting there waiting for the next shot and Jackie would just often disappear, and know body knew where he was. He would often just go off to his office to try and figure out what the next scene was going to be. I remember one day he got a delivery from Mitsubishi, this new sports car; he was always getting gifts and Mitsubishi was one of his big donors it seemed and he would call out "Vincent, Vincent have a look at my new car" and it had this flashy computer on board, and remember this was long before the cars you see today have this on board. He would also be playing Game Boy, dancing listening to music. So there would be days go by twelve, fourteen hours where I would just be sitting around in this horrible make-up.

RB – I am guessing that only Jackie could get away with this, he is at his peak he can command a large budget unlike other Hong Kong stars at the time so I am guessing no one bothered him.

VL – Yes, and of course he was by now well over budget and the studio wanted him to finish as they were hoping for a summer opening that was not going to work, how about a Christmas opening? I think finally it was set for a Chinese New Year opening. Now at the time I was

filming two other movies "Robo-trix. (I pipe up with the lovely Amy yip) Vincent smiles and nods his head. And "Fury in Red" with "Philip Ko" "Robin Shou" and "Wang Lung Wei" and Jackie calls up and talks to Wang and said "You got to kill Vincent off, I don't care how you do it but you got to kill him off because he is in my movie in the main fight scene and I

cannot afford for him to have an accident or any injuries" so basically I get killed off! And actually I was supposed to be a lead in that film all the way through.

RB – So back you went?

VL – Yep, remembers the first day of shooting Chris Lee and a bunch of the other JC stuntmen and they had worked out some choreography. And I spent like half an hour to get it down, and of course Jackie walks over and says "Ok, show me the choreography". So I am working with Chris Lee back and forth and you hear Jackie say "No, No, No, I don't like it" he then basally steps in changes the choreography. Let me say that when I was working with Jackie it felt like I had two left feet and remember I had done now nearly Two dozen films in Hong Kong I was sure that I had the knack of this when it comes to the fight choreography but I think doing this in front of Jackie for the first time I felt nervous.

RB – So was Jackie doing all the choreography for the film?

VL – Well even though the JC stunt group were doing the fight scenes, but a lot of the time he took on many roles, this is why they call it "Jackie's Apocalypse Now" He basically takes on every main role from lead actor to Director to martial arts stunt choreographer he was doing everything.

RB – Apparently it's only when he is being directed by his big brother Sammo Hung that he takes a bit of a back seat.

VL – yes sounds right, but after a few days of being on set you start to get combatable with the rhythm of the way Jackie does things and it was a different experience to anybody else I had worked with and he can be quite goofy on set but always a perfectionist doing these takes sometime thirty to forty times. Also he can seem very relaxed and calm and he is very helpful when he is directing you. So over a few days I kind of just gelled.

RB – That's good because you know he is trying not only to get the best out of you but also that you will look good when you watch it on the big screen.

VL – That is right, he really does do that for you and caring about making you and every one on screen look the best they can and not just himself.

RB – did you know Steve Tartalia, Bruce Fontaine, Ken Goodman and Wayne Archer before you made this movie?

VL – Yes of course from filming in Hong Kong.

RB – I have heard some shocking stories (laughing)

Page 92   Eastern Heroes Jackie Chan Special Edition

be practicing his "Eagle Claw" on set and Jackie would say "stop doing that! There is no Kung Fu in this film it's just fighting not period style" and you know Steve, he is a great guy but he can be kind of frenetic and looks nervous, which in turn can start to make everybody else nervous and the scene in which he is going to be killed off in is where I throw Steve the key and he starts to turn the key and he always gives some good advice to the crew and he will take a look at some of the shots give feedback.

RB – this would have been before you went you did Armour of God 2 right?

VL – Yes I had seen Jackie before

RB - Because Jackie meets so many people I wondered if he had remembered he can be forgetful like that.

VL – well talking about forgetting, going forward I saw Jackie here in New York when he came to do a book signing of his book and I decided to go and there was a humbling moment when he was signing and he saw me and it was a cold day so I was wearing a big duffel coat, and he got up "wow Vincent" actually Jackie always pronounced my name "Wincent" still was not able to say my name

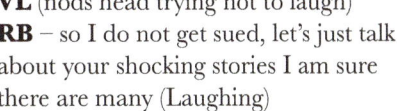

VL (nods head trying not to laugh)

RB – so I do not get sued, let's just talk about your shocking stories I am sure there are many (Laughing)

VL – yes, tons of stories Steve in particular who you know well, you know when he is around something is going to happen and it may not be good (laughing). Jackie comes up to me and says "Steve he makes me very nervous I am going to kill him off today" Steve you know, would and the gun turrets are pointing at him, and if you freeze frame that moment, the look on his face, he was pissed because he had been telling everyone he was going to be in the last scene it was not a good moment.

RB – Was you there when Jackie comes on to the set of "Outlaw Brothers"?

VL – yes, he visited a couple of times maybe to see how the film was going but maybe more because he was a gig brother to Frankie Chan

properly (laughing) and it was really nice to see him.
But going back to Armour of God 2 a moment I remember kind of funny was the Wind tunnel scene which took about 40 days or more to shoot.
RB – It was really that long to film.
VL – yes, about forty days and forty nights!
RB – for like a 3 or four minute scene.
VL – yes.
RB - So shooting so much footage was there much left on the cutting room floor?
VL – The original Hong Kong? No it was pretty much everything
RB – OK!
VL – And you know the scenes where we are all harnessed up and start flying around and there is a lot of wind, but it was not the wind due to the turbine fan, that moved very slowly and was sped up. But to create the wind effect they were using like industrial big industrial fans and the guys would use like "Air Hoses" and of course with all the make-up on my face these hoses would like tear away at my make-up, so every day the make-up would look slightly different it would never be exactly the same.
RB – So no continuity then
VL – no, No, No there was ANY continuity (laughs) so as I was being catapulted through the air, sometimes the wire would snap so they would have to harness me up again and changed the tension of the wire and sometimes I would not be moving fast enough so they would gather like three or four guys and remember there is no physics behind this and eventually you could end up with ten guys yanking the ropes. So as I am flying through the air and it's always the same you do it correct in rehearsal and then the minute the cameras are rolling and I would forget to tuck my head down and when there is ten guys yanking you across the screen of course my head whips back and ends up cracking a slat on impact. So there is Jackie on the podium

with four Panavision cameras at the same time trying to get the right shot.
RB – That is almost unknown back then to use four Panavision comers on a film set it would blow the budget!
VL – Yes, you're talking about a Million dollars' worth of camera equipment because Jackie wants to make sure he has got every angle and every shot.
RB – And recently at the "Fighting Spirit Film festival" they screened the new 88 film print and it did look good.
VL – Oh really that must have been great, I do actually have a copy of it that they sent me which I will get round to looking at.
RG Jackie back then always wanted his films to open for Chines New year, to get the maximum audience as history shows Chinese New Year openings create a bigger box office return.
LV – that is correct, he wanted an extra two million dollars U.S he wanted to shoot the car scenes with the Rene Julian stunt team so that was another two million added to the already over budget movie
RB – So, one last question, When did you first see the final cut of the movie on the big screen
VL – Well I saw it at the premier in Hong Kong, in fact my parents flew over to join me, I also attended the American premier when Miramax brought the movie in July 97 and it premiered at "The Cinemas Ziegfeld Theatre" here in New York and they held an after party at the "China Grill" and in fact I was the only person of the cast that was there I went with Ric Myers with Weinstein behind me Jet Li and his wife were to my right there was a lot of people there from the movies and then when the lights went down Jackie came in and he sat right behind us But I will tell you, Miramax really botched the edit of that.
RB – yes I talked to Brett Ratner who was responsible for turning Jackie into a huge worldwide success with the massive box office opening for "Rush Hour" and he had said that about all the American re issues.

VL – It was really bad and Jackie let me tell you was pissed he was really upset and it showed at the after party and I believe he did not want to take a photo with anybody. He came up to Ric and me and said "Man they really ruined my movie! What the hell did they do to it" they had cut I think sixteen, seventeen minutes out they had put a new soundtrack that I thought was not to bad and enhanced the colourisation of the movie. What made it worse was that in the television previews they were actually using shots from the original film that was not in the new cut which for me did not make any sense. Luckily I got a couple of photos with him and I think I was the only person who he let have a picture taken of him with someone. And just to end this I believe I actually heard this story that Steve who told me! The story, he tried to get into the premier so I told Ric I am going to bring a lady I will bring another beautiful lady for you so the four of us. So we get a limousine we pull up red carpet and all the networks are there this was really a major thing, and the lines of people I mean it was just going around the block. Now I heard that Steve was trying to get in! He went to the front of the line of course there are police officers everywhere and he said "Hey! I am in the movie" and of course they just look at him with that of course you look and said "If you're in the movie then why are you trying to cut in line". So he tries to force his way in and one of the officers grabs his arm and Steve turns round and does some kind of Chi-Nah Lock (Vincent laughing Hysterically) so

Vincent with Rick's mum

another cop comes in and they ARREST HIM (Vincent still laughing). So what Steve told me was that "Wow that was good what was that you just did on me. So of course I am hearing this from Steve so who knows how much fact but knowing Steve I probably believed it to be true

RB (laughing along with the story because I know Steve too well) Vincent its been great chatting to you and as always these talks can go long into the night but thank you so much for spending a little time with me, I always see you jetting off around the world sitting in some first call business lounge so I caught you at the right time. But really thank you for sharing few stories the readers will love it and maybe in 2022 you might come to the UK?

VL – Rick if you get Cynthia over for a show I will jump on a plane and come join her and you can screen "Blonde Fury".

RB It's a deal

成龍

THE PROFESSIONAL COLLECTOR
Sneak Peak

In this section we have the opportunity to get a sneak peak at Paul Dre's personal collection. Founder of the Jackie Chan Apperciation Group on facebook, Paul has an extensive collection ranging from films, figures, toys, consoles and even lifesize cardboard cutouts of Jackie. Hopefully we will get a larger article dedicated to Paul's collection in future Eastern Heroes magazines, but for now, enjoy the next couple of pages.

ANDY CHENG 鄭繼宗

MAN ON A MISSION
執行任務的人

By Rick baker

Actor, Stuntman, Choreographer, Director and a member of the Jackie Chan Stunt team from the Late 1990's to the early 2000's and most importantly super nice talented guy!
Mini-Bioa Cheng Kai-Chung better

known as Andy Cheng was born in Hong Kong. At the age of 14, he began studying the Korean martial art of Tae Kwon Do. He won three gold medals at the Hong Kong Invitational from 1988 to 1990, followed by a bronze medal at the 1991 Asian Games. He would retire from competition to start his career in the film industry. n 1990, Cheng was discovered by legendary filmmaker Lau Kar-leung and had a small role as a Tae Kwon Do instructor in New Kids in Town. From there, Andy spent the next five years working at TVB, owned and operated by the Shaw Brothers. He would then be invited to join the Jackie Chan Stunt Team and serve as a stuntman and occasional double for Chan himself when needed. This would lead Cheng to appear in prominent henchman roles in films like Rush Hour and Rush Hour 2 while doubling for Chan in films like Who Am I? And, Mr Nice Guy.

In 2001, Cheng was loaned out to director Isaac Florentine to ramp up the action sequences and serve as lead fight choreographer on U.S. Seals II: The Ultimate Force. In addition to fight choreography, Andy appeared in the film as Artie, a blonde-haired henchman to Damian Chapa's villain character. This led to Cheng eventually forming his own team, with martial artist and assistant Dan South worth as his assistant on films like The Scorpion King and The Rundown, both starring Dwayne Johnson with Cheng serving as the stunt coordinator and fight choreographer on these films.

In 2006, Cheng made his feature film directorial debut on End Game, a political thriller starring Cuba Gooding Jr. A year later, he followed that up with the car racing film Redline, starring Nathan Phillips and Nadia Bjorlin. Cheng was the stunt coordinator for the 2008 hit adaptation of Stephanie Meyer's acclaimed youth adult novel Twilight. Cheng has since worked steadily as a stunt coordinator in both television and films since and more recently work as Fight Coordinator on Shang-Chi and the Legend of the Ten Rings.

I caught up with Andy recently to chat about his work with Jackie Chan
RB Hi Andy, How are you?
AC Oh it's been crazy, I have been doing so many interviews since the release on Shang-Chi and the Legend of the Ten Rings
RB so you worked on "Rush Hour 1 and 2 but not number 3?
AC No, I was directing another project at the time so he replied well you better be ready if we shoot number 4! so I said Ok just let me know when, because you are my lucky charm. I have been waiting for this so I hope at some stage it happens.
RB do you think that Jackie might be a bit to old now to revive his character?
AC Not really, I think right now with all

he technology they could easily use face replacement for certain scenes but Jackie is still able to do things.

RB well I hope so, because I saw photos of Sammo Hung and he was at that time using a walking stick and he did not look in such good shape, I think he can still direct or act but fighting might be asking a lot.

AC sometimes you see him in a wheel chair, but this is not because he cannot walk, I think he tries to save energy and he tries to save his Knee, but for fighting he would definitely need a double so today's technology can go a long way to keeping these stars on screen, even Bruce Lee who has been gone a long time still with the new technology we could see him back on screen.

RB I think so! But I read on line that at a recent conference they asked if he would make a fourth part of "The Rush Hour" franchise and he said "Yes! But please soon as I am getting old"

AC yes! Brett please do number 4 before I am to old (laughing)

RB I asked Brett that if "Rush Hour 4" went ahead would he bring in two new actors like Sylvester Stallone handed over the baton to Jason Statham to continue the "Expendable" franchise. But Brett said "No, No it must be Jackie and Chris should it ever happen.

AC No, I agree it should be with Jackie and Chris, you cannot replace these two

RB So, back to "Rush Hour" what is your memory if how this project got off the ground?

AC yes! So Jackie was filming "Who am I?" in South Africa and Jackie knew Brett was coming to pitch him a script he made a long trip to meet with Jackie in Johannesburg to meet Jackie for just one day and he impressed Jackie and that really is the start of how "rush hour" got made. Jackie came up to me and said "When I finish this movie (Who am I?) I will go to Hollywood, will you come with me?" of course and that is how I started doing two films for Jackie and then I move to America to work on "Rush Hour".

RB what was it like working on "Rush Hour"? because Brett at that time maybe he realised but when Jackie is on set, unless he is with Sammo Hung, Jackie he takes control of the movie and Brett at this stage had not really got any experience with this type of action movie except a lot of passion and love for his project and Jackie.

AC yes! This story I have spoken about when we arrived to film "Rush hour" we were very polite Jackie I remember when we started shooting Jackie was very quiet and polite to every department the DP and Brad Allen who has very sadly now passed away.

RB I know that was such a shock to read that on Facebook such a talented guy.

AC yes this was very sad to me I had spoken to him recently before this happened I felt very sad.

RB me too, I never met him but appreciated his work. So what happened next?

AC well we had been shooting for about two weeks, and the schedule was getting worse with Brett at this stage not controlling the situation so well but was learning fast, and we came to do the sequence where he says "hey what's up *******". And that fight scene in the whore house we are outside, waiting for the shooting inside where they are gambling and we have been waiting all day and we now have only three hours left! And we want to do the fight scene and they come out and say we have to cut the fight scene down to just three hours. So, Jackie now we have been waiting so long gets upset about this and this is the first time he says "If this is going to end up like "Battle Creek Brawl, or "Cannon Ball Run "like those kind of stupid movies again! I am not going to let this movie ruin my career" so now he is very upset and he goes inside to talk to Brett and "we do it or not" and then the DP comes and he has a big fight with him. Finally! Brett says "OK, let's let him try his way, Jackie is a big star and knows what he is doing". So in three hours we came up with that whole sequence. So then, because the DP was upset we kicked the

"rush Hour 2" nobody touches anything with the action. So it was the whore house, this was the moment things changed

RB it's true you can see the change of pace in the movie.

AC Yes Jackie really fights for his career and from that moment things got better

RB So, what is the rehearsals like with Jackie? Are they worked out over a couple of days or does Jackie figures the fight sequences out there and then?

AC when Jackie goes on set there is no rehearsal, we have some idea before, but when Jackie arrives we always listen to him and do what he asks of us, he is the one that knows what he can do and also his stunt team

RB if I was doing a film with Jackie and there was a fight sequence to be filmed, I would just say Jackie off you go I will just make sure the camera is pointing the right way because for those of us that have followed Jackie we know, in this department he is a genius (laughing)

AC we pose a few ideas to Jackie, but weather Jackie takes the ideas or not, he will always work out the whole sequence by himself. So that why we don't rehearse until Jackie arrives. It's just like you see in the behind the scenes at the end of the movie (the outtakes) like the scene in the Chinese restaurant and there is me and Jackie and he grabs my hand "oh let's try this" and we try and it works so he is creating and trying ideas all the time for what he thinks will look best for the action.

RB so the choreography is very spontaneous then?

AC Yes! He will try something and teach you and say "OK! This is what we will do" and then Brett will say "How about this" and so we try his idea to.

RB So, Brett still had some input?

AC Yes! Brett will say something and Jackie will go "Ok" and then he tries something else and this will be how a concept will be formed and then ok let's shoot. And it's all about trying to make th scene smooth weather it be Jacki or Chris it has to work and look good on the playback.

RB back in the days of the early Jackie films, Jackie was lucky to be afforded to take many, many takes to get a scene right. So wha about with "Rush Hour" did you have to do many takes?

AC often we did many, many takes! Jackie and Brett know wha they want so neither of them would compromise. Before in Jackie's earlier films they would take many shots but with "Rush hour" and Jackie's experience it was a much easier task.

RB I offend wondered when I saw Hong Kong actors going to film in America, how they would adapt having shot movies Hong Kong style and now filming American style with the insurance companies watching over them and the way they were used to filming in Hong Kong. I remember an American camera man saying he did not understand the wa Hong Kong movies were shot with the fight sequences with all the speeding up and all the different angles. And I often wondered back in the day how it would work out when you fused Hong Kong action being shot in an American movie with their very set ways and health and safety because in Hong Kong I can refer to a saying when filming "Life is cheap, but toilet paper is expensive" (laughing)

AC Yes of course! But he realises that there is health and safety. We know there are guide lines but we still try to make the scene with good action, and know were the camera needs to be and we still know were to hide a mat and to create a good scene without risk. in Hong Kong they wi often do a big wire master scene but we still no even shooting in America how to create this and no when to cut and make

ANDY CHENG
STUNT CO-ORDINATOR

DP out and this allowed us to complete the sequence and from that moment we take control and Brett said "you see he can do fast and good!" so we still all work together with the DP but after that we had more control as Brett now understands how Jackie works. Then when we do

the action safe.

RB so when did you become part of Jackie's Stunt team, I notice you're wearing one of the JC Stunt team when you have finished with that please ship it to me (Smiling)

AC It was soon as I finished filming "Mr Nice Guy" that I joined his Stunt Group and of course after filming "Who am I" he wanted me to come to America with him.

RB so what generation of the stunt team was it when you joined

AC it was the fourth generation I think now it's up to the 9th generation usually changes every five years so soon be the 10th generation starting its 50th years so new Stunt group will be added

RB Must be a dream to be a part of his stunt group, so for the readers can you give me a good story from either "Rush Hour 1 or 2 "

AC Yes, well people will now know this story, it was when I almost died filming the boat scene and Jackie saved me. We are in the middle of the harbour we get a midnight phone call and we had no safety diver to use under the water, and we do the fight scene and it means that it requires a stuntman to fall into the water with a moving Current and it is the scene were John Lone's character falls into the water. She fakes shooting him, and he falls into the water but he survives so it was a fake kill. My stunt brother falls in for John and during that test we had under water safety, it is night time and this stunt is very scary. So next day we are doing choreography for a fight scene on the boat and Jackie says "hey! Why don't someone fall in the

water" and I always wanted to do this as a stunt! Because to me I think it's and fun! So when we try this Jackie says let's try two people and one is supposed to grab the other by the hand and both fall in. One of the stunt guys my brother a young Korean Boy said he was scared and did not want to try it as he had injured himself on another stunt and his leg was sore and also I am not good with swimming! So I said do not worry I will double you in this scene, so I double the stunt guy and when he is supposed to fall I swap over and fall in. When we both fall in one guy is now on top of me! And the current is moving and the boat is still moving and about 10 seconds later I emerged from the water and I say WOW that was fun! And the boat came to pick us up and Jackie says "ok good, go get change and we try one more" he liked the shot but said to Brett let's do one more! So he asked me when you do this next time can you just arch your back over the boat as the guy falls over you. Easy" I said so Jackie runs back and says "Ok! Action" and the camera start to film. BUT! I arch my back I keep arching and I end up falling into the water and now it's five, ten seconds and I still have not come out of the water and then I hit the boat with my head and I realise I have fallen under the boat and I think OH! I am going to die because of the boats propeller whirling close to me. I cannot see its black down there and it is midnight, and I cannot open my eyes and now I am spinning, spinning like a back roll and my head keeps hitting the boat at the same time I am trying to grab something but the underneath of the boat is so slimy and I am holding my breath and start saying "Andy Cheng, Andy Cheng" this is not fun anymore this was meant to be someone else's stunt. By now I am stating to suck water and I think about my daughter that has just been born, and I think I do not have my son yet so I cannot DIE!! So I try not to panic as I hold my breath someone will come. But I keep sucking in the water and I am still spinning. I was told that at that moment they were still looking for me they see

ANDY CHENG

- Director/Fight Coordinator/Martial Artist/Stunt Coordinator
- Jackie Chan Stunt Team Member
- Movie/TV Credits: Shang-Chi, Shanghai Noon, Rush Hour, Rush Hour 2, Martial Law, The Scorpion King, The New World, The Run Down, Red Riding Hood, Twilight, Into Badlands, 6 Underground, Endgame, Redline

First Bruce Lee Foundation Award Winner, 2021

one guy who has come up away from the boat so they think I am going to be in that area. But for me by now I am starting to give up my body is shutting down and suddenly I feel a hand come down and grab me and I think please do not let go as I try to hold on to them and as they bring me up I realise that the hand that grabbed me belong to Jackie. I was so lucky because if it had been another star on that film I do not think they would have found me. Why everyone was looking out at the water for me Jackie looks down and see's my Jacket so he realises I am under the boat so he just reaches in and pulls me out. Also I was lucky because the boat had a Jet Ski platform and meant I was not that far down like a normal boat meaning Jackie could lean over and pull me out had the boat been bigger I would not have been seen. But let me tell you that Jackie's hands are so huge and strong that he could grab me like a claw and pull me up for that I am so lucky! so three lucky things that saved my life!

RB Wow what a story obviously someone was watching over you at that moment. Before we end this as like always we can chat till the cows come home have you got any dream projects you would like to direct?

AC I have a few one I will talk about with you later, I would love to remake "Wheels on Meals" and try to find a new Jackie, Sammo and Yuen Biao. I love this film and if the opportunity arises this would be my dream project.

RB Andy if that happens I will be sitting in the front row at the premier, DO IT!! Thanks you again for chatting and I am sure we will do another interview on your upcoming projects

AC thank you Ricky

A Brief History of the VCD

For those of you have been collecting Hong Kong films for many years, the VCD will be a well known format. The compact disc was originally introduced in 1982 by a collaboration from Phillips and Sony to digitise sound, soon the idea of using this format for video using the same technology laser discs use to create the Video CD in 1987. Initially only 5 minutes of video could fit onto a disc due to the size being much more compact than a 12" laserdisc. By 1990 however the technology improved meaning more storage could be utilised with the compression of video signals meant that a single disc could now store up to 40 minutes of video, and 2 discs would be required for a single film. Some extra capacity could be made with a small drop in quality of video, this explains why some VCD's don't appear to be as sharp as some VHS films. Although Viseo CD was most popular in Asia, the format was briefly available in the US and also some parts of Europe but surprisingly not Japan. The format started to die out with the introduction of CD-R discs and recorders, meaning copying was extremely easy and an exact copy could be made for next to nothing. Then along came the DVD and blew the VCD out of the water with a much higher storage capacity for better quality video on each disc. As my sources go, VCD's were still available up until 2013 possibly in Tailand, but as of now the format is very much the collectors market.

With all the above being said, and the fact that the quality of the VCD can be very low on some releases, it still remains close to my heart, being the go to format personally for me once the VHS had run its course. The appeal of the VCD was a no brainer, no longer was there a bulky case and fairly large tape to store, but a small case the same size as an audio CD would fit nicely on my shelf and the fact that the quality would not degrade like VHS or potentially get ruined by a faulty player was a bif bonus. A trip London China Town a few times a month gave me ample time to go into the handful of shops selling VCD's at around £10 each back in the late 90's and into the 2000's. The fact that these were reasonably cheap made them all the more appealing. Now, as this is a Jackie special edition of the Eastern Heroes magazine, I will be displaying some of the variable artwork on different releases of some films and also some internal artwork and picture discs and maybe some rare images not often seen. As with most Hong Kong films there are various releases with different accompanying artwork. So I hope you enjoy the following ages as a small display of some the artwork that accompanies Jackies films.

少林木人巷
SHAOLIN WOODEN MEN

警察故事
POLICE STORY

龍兄虎弟
ARMOUR OF GOD

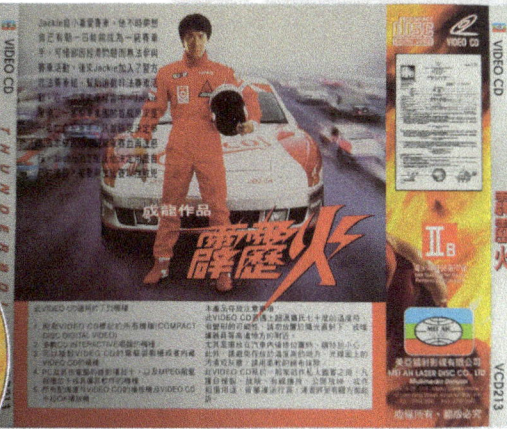

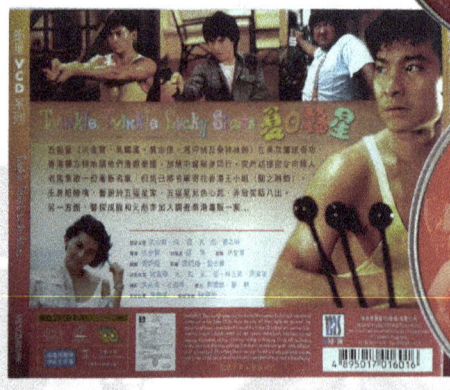

警察故事
POLICE STORY 3 (aka SUPERCOP)

舞台姊妹
STAGE DOOR JOHNNY

Page 113 Eastern Heroes Jackie Chan Special Edition

特務迷城
THE ACCIDENTAL SPY

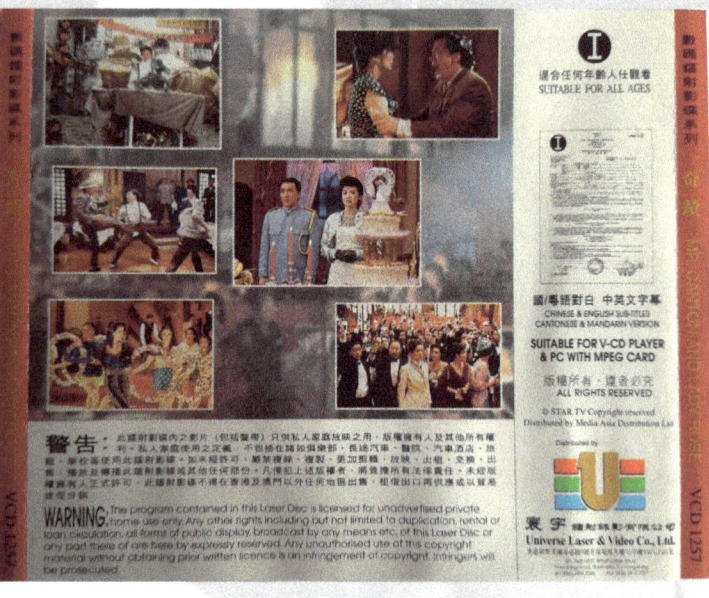

奇蹟
MR CANTON & LADY ROSE
(AKA MIRACLES)

警察故事
POLICE STORY 2

超級計劃
PROJECT S

Page 115 Eastern Heroes Jackie Chan Special Edition

火燒島
ISLAND OF FIRE

威龍猛探
THE PROTECTOR

福星高照
MY LUCKY STARS

醉拳
DRUNKEN MASTER

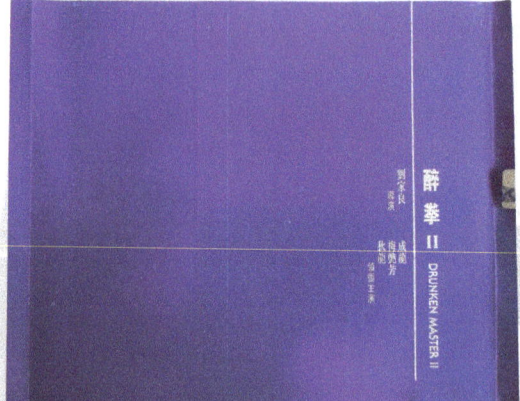
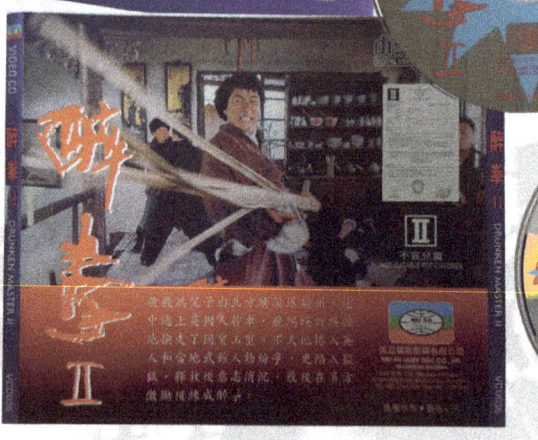

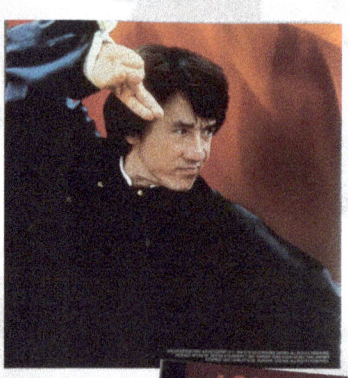
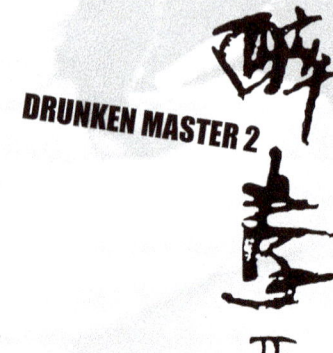

重案組
CRIME STORY

www.ingramcontent.com/pod-product-compliance
Lightning Source LLC
Chambersburg PA
CBHW051307110526
44589CB00025B/2967